Life in the Minors
5th Annual Phillies Minor League Digest

By Steve Potter & Larry Shenk

D1501698

Foreword
By
Tom McCarthy

Photo by Miles Kennedy

The first day of the Minor League baseball season in Trenton in 1994 was an amazing event on so many levels. For me, it changed my life and changed the life of my family. But it actually never happened. It was 5:30 in the morning and I was walking out to the outfield at Trenton's Waterfront Park with our General Manager, and my good friend, Wayne Hodes. As we walked on the outfield grass, we sank about a half of foot each time we took a step. We were about to do a live shot to promote the opening of our new stadium. Trenton had a great history of minor league baseball but hadn't had a team in 44 years. It was a dream come true for so many who grew up going to Dunn Field in Trenton to see Willie Mays and who flipped on the radio to hear eventual Hall of Fame sportswriter, Bus Saidt, do the play by play for those same Trenton Giants. I was excited because I had never done a professional game until 1994. I had done college and high school games, where I strung phone wire 100 yards at a time to get a signal. Now I was beginning my journey to the big leagues, 20 minutes from where I went to college.

For me, my time with the Thunder was a great education on the history of Minor League Baseball in the city of Trenton. How Willie Mays made his professional debut with the Giants and was taken under the wing of Giants outfielder Mo Cunningham, who eventually settled in Hamilton, NJ, when his playing career finished. I felt connected to all of those teams. Just as this book is a great history lesson of minor league baseball within the Phillies family. Larry and Steve wind us through not only the different cities that have made up the family tree, but it also connects the fans to the minor leaguers who, past and present, make up the lineage of the Phillies family.

That day in April of 1994 was just the beginning for me in Minor League Baseball. It was also just the beginning for my family, which was growing with each passing year. On that day in 1994, we never played at Waterfront Park. The Yankees farm team, from Albany, was scheduled to be the opponent of the Trenton Thunder – the Double-A affiliate of the Detroit Tigers. But they wouldn't play on the unplayable field. They made the right decision. The field was too wet, even though there was no rain. That night, though, with a packed crowd still at Waterfront Park, we announced the postponement. The players, sensing the fans were disappointed, started to go through the crowd, saying hello and signing autographs. They were led by eventual Major

Leaguer and current Major League Baseball Players Association President, Tony Clark. Tony and I remain good friends today, and it all began that year. Friendships like that are what I remember most about my time in the minors.

I spent seven years in the minor leagues as the radio and television broadcaster, media relations director, and eventually the Assistant General Manager of the Thunder. During my time as an executive, I pulled tarp, swept up garbage, raked the field, cleaned the clubhouse, sold advertising – which I never liked – arranged travel for players and their families, wore the mascot costume, made hot dogs, fixed toilets and made a ton of friends. It was truly the greatest education I have ever had in my life. It has led me to where I am today. It also planted the seed for my two sons, one who is already in the Triple A broadcast booth at the age of 25 and the other, trying to navigate his way through Independent Baseball as a ballplayer. They know the meaning of a strong minor league team and what it does to a community. Working in Trenton opened my eyes to some of the most talented people in the world of baseball, many of whom are still in the minor leagues for the same reason I was there: For the love of the game, the laughter of families and to bring community happiness to an area in need of a sports identity.

For years, Steve Potter has given us a look at the Phillies farm system with an energy that no one else has displayed. Steve not only has a love for the Phillies, which is evident in his writing, but also his relationships with the many minor leaguers who have come through the Phillies organization. Now, with the great Larry Shenk – an icon in Philadelphia sports and within the Phillies family – the two have combined their passion for baseball, knowledge, and love of Phillies, to put together a great road map of the Phillies minor league history. Not only giving us a glimpse of the players, but of the cities that have housed those players.

But it's not just a look at the players or managers you know, it's a look at the characters who helped make some of the iconic Phillies players who they became, like Bill Dancy, the long-time Phillies minor league coach and coordinator who managed some of the great Phillies who became part of the 2008 championship team. Or long-time manager/coach, Greg Legg, who is one of the most successful managers in the Phillies minor league history. Greg and I first met when I was with the Thunder and some years later our relationship came full circle when my son, Patrick, broadcast for Reading and Lehigh Valley, while Greg was managing and coaching those teams. Pretty incredible.

One of my favorite parts of the book is the description of the more than 100 different Minor League affiliations the Phillies have had over the years. From Hazleton in the New York Penn League, to Scranton/Wilkes-Barre in the International League. One of my favorite hats growing up was the triangle Scranton hat the Phillies wore when they played as the Red Barons. Larry and Steve give you a thumbnail of the stadiums that were the centerpiece of some towns and the timeline of each of these affiliations.

There are also stories of hope, and the simplicity of Minor League Baseball. The time that our former Director of Team Travel, Frank Coppenbarger, had an at bat in a Minor League game, while handling the clubhouse duties. It is reminiscent of the time Bob Feller, in full uniform, sat in my office <u>from 10 a.m.</u> until game time, signing autographs, editorializing my phone conversations, and critiquing my lunch order. This was the life of a Minor League Baseball executive. You never knew what your day would be like.

Skim it, consume it, talk about it, and pass it on. Minor League baseball is the heartbeat of baseball. Its history is not just important to preserve, it's important to understand and keep fresh in everyone's mind. Because like everything else, Minor League Baseball is changing, not only for the Phillies, but for each of the towns that make up our organization's great history.

Table of Contents

Preface

After the 2016 minor league season concluded I published my first book detailing the Phillies system and many player performances. The following three seasons, with the help of some very skilled writers and photographers, we published what we envisioned to become an annual minor league digest reflecting on the season that had just passed. The joint venture has become a passion for our collective group and we enjoyed gifting our work to multiple players and their families, friends in the media and the Phillies organization. We envisioned producing the digest for many years to come.

Then the pandemic came. We were at Carpenter Complex the day the 2020 minor league spring training camp was terminated, and the players were sent home. We stood outside the gate as the fellas came out in dismay that their season would be interrupted indefinitely, and their futures put in disarray. Our chats were brief that day. We all hoped it would be a short interruption and wished each other well till the group reconvened to resume play.

A few months later as we were all immersed in the lockdown of life as we knew it word came that the minor league season had been cancelled. It was disappointing news for all to hear.

Opportunities often arise from disappointment, with no season to chronicle a digest I began to research the history of Phillies minor league baseball. I've learned things that quite frankly I likely would not have taken the time had the season continued.

It's been my good fortune to get to know Larry (Baron) Shenk the past few years as well. When I began writing Phillies minor league notes a few years back, it's been my privilege to share them with various Phillies personnel, both active and retired. Baron even enlisted me to write articles on Phillies Insider during spring training. He's been a great mentor and advisor since I've delved into my post-retirement hobby of writing about Phillies minor league baseball.

He called me one day after reading a few of the articles I had written about the Phillies minor league history and suggested that it would make a good book, one that had never been done before. He even stated that he would partner in the endeavor. That's how this book came to fruition. We've entitled it "Life in the Minors" and it has now filled the void of having no season. We've enlisted it as the fifth annual digest … representative of the 2020 Phillies minor league season that didn't exist by documenting the history of the sites, people, and events of the various ones that came before.

Sometimes opportunity comes in unanticipated ways … It's All Part of It. We hope you enjoy this year's digest. We look forward to returning next season with the 6th digest when our players take the field once more.

Steve Potter

Tenure and the Beginning

Minor League History

Minor league baseball has been around since 1902. A lot of changes have taken place over time--the number of leagues, different classifications, and communities with teams. Minor league teams were owned and operated completely independent of major league clubs in the beginning. They signed players and sold them to the majors.

Minor league players were also subjected to the "Selection of Players" draft which officially became the Rule 5 draft n 1941. The Phillies, in 1910, drafted RHP Grover Cleveland Alexander from Syracuse. He wound up in the Hall of Fame. General Manager Branch Rickey of the St. Louis Cardinals is credited with the idea of having a farm system, working agreements with minor league teams. It happened in 1930. The Phillies first minor league affiliate, according to baseball-reference.com, was in Hazleton (PA), the Mountaineers of the Class A, New York Penn League, 1934-36. They had no affiliate in 1937 but two the next year, Montgomery (AL) Rebels (Class B, Southern League) and Centreville (MD) Colts (Class D, Eastern Shore League).

The greatest number of Phillies minor league teams was 15 in both 1948 and 1949. Baseball had 59 leagues and 448 minor league teams in 1949, an all-time high.

Since Hazleton, the Phillies have had over 100 affiliates in communities scattered across the country and Canada. The longest tenured:

Reading (PA), Phillies/Fightin Phils (53 years)
Clearwater (FL), Phillies/Threshers (35)
Clearwater, (FL), GCL, Phillies/East/West (22)
Spartanburg (SC), Phillies/Traders/Spinners/Suns (22)
Batavia (NY), Trojans/Clippers/Muckdogs (20)
Lakewood (NJ), Blue Claws (19)
Williamsport (PA), Crosscutters (18)
Scranton/Wilkes-Barre (PA), Red Barons (18)
Pulaski (VA), Counts/Phillies (13)
Allentown (PA), Lehigh Valley Iron Pigs (12)
Bradford, (PA), Blue Wings (12)
Schenectady (NY), Blue Jays (12)

Jack Russell Stadium – Clearwater – courtesy of Larry Shenk

Jack Russell Memorial Stadium was the home of the Phillies first minor league team in Clearwater. Under manager Ramon Aviles, the Clearwater Phillies played their first Florida State League game against the Tampa Tarpons at home on April 12, 1985.

Four players on that roster made it to the majors, 1B Ricky Jordan, RHP Marvin Freeman, LHP Wally Ritchie, and LHP Bruce Ruffin.

Cranberry Park, Hazelton, PA - Courtesy, cranberrycreek.org

Hazleton Mountaineers

The very first Phillies minor league affiliation was with the Hazleton (PA) Mountaineers (1934-1936). Hazleton was one of eight teams in the New York-Penn League, then a Class A league.

The Mountaineers were first formed on June 16, 1929 when the Syracuse Stars moved to Hazleton on an emergency basis because their stadium collapsed. Hazleton competed in the New York–Penn League through 1932, was inactive in 1933, and revived the following season as an affiliate of the Phillies.

Two other major league clubs followed, Boston Red Sox (1937–1938) and the Brooklyn Dodgers (1950).

Over time Hazleton was in the NYPL (1929-32; 1937), Eastern League (1938), Interstate League (1939-40), and North Atlantic League (1949-50). When the NAL folded following the 1950 season, minor league baseball in Hazleton ended.

Ballpark
Cranberry Ball Park: The Hazleton Coal Company, founded in 1836, was the initial owner of the site. The majority of the property was used for anthracite coal mining. The ball field occupied part of the site (1922-1965) until State Route 924 was constructed through the property. The site is now included in the Cranberry Creek Gateway Project established in 2006 with the intention of developing 366 acres into a residential and commercial community.

1934: **Manager**: Frank Uzmann ... 61-75, 7th place.

Eight players on the roster had or would spend time in the majors. RHP Hal Kelleher, who made his pro debut, had the longest tenure in the majors, parts of four seasons with the Phillies (1935-38). He's in the team's record book, ignominiously, for allowing the most runs in an inning: 12, 8th inning, at the Chicago Cubs in 21-2 loss, May 5, 1938. It was his last day in the majors.

1935: **Player-Manager**: Andy High ... 74-56, 3rd place.

Ten players had major league service. Longest were LHP Russ Bauers, eight seasons, and OF Morrie Arnovich, who wound up playing five of his seven seasons with the Phillies (1936-

40). 37-year-old Andy High was the third baseman-manager. His 13-year-career in the majors ended with 47 games with the 1934 Phillies. He later became the Director of Scouting for the Brooklyn/LA Dodgers, a position he held until he retired in 1963.

1936: **Managers**: Andy High, George Tice, Joe O'Rourke, Frank Uzmann ... 66-72, 6th place.

INF Rod Dedeaux played 42 games for the Mountaineers, one of four minor league seasons. His big-league experience consisted of two games with the 1935 Brooklyn Dodgers. He went on to become the winningest coach in college baseball history (1,332-571) at USC, winning 11 College World Series.

RHP Hugh Mulcahy, 22, had a phenomenal season, 25-14, on a team that won only 66 games. It is doubtful any Phillies minor leaguer pitcher ever won that many games again. He pitched in the majors for nine seasons of which eight were with the Phillies. He gained national distinction when he became the first major leaguer to be drafted into the military before the U.S. entered World War II, on March 8, 1941. Mulcahy ended up serving over four years.

Miners Declare a Holiday Only to See Ruth Fan Twice

HAZELTON, Pa., Oct. 22.—Babe Ruth came to Hazleton today for a baseball game. It was made a holiday, the mines and the public schools of all towns in the region closing for the afternoon. Mine workers left their posts in such numbers that work had to be suspended. Babe went hitless against Mondero, a mine worker of Coleraine, who pitched for the Hazleton team. He struck the home run king out twice.

The New York Times
Published: October 23, 1923
Copyright © The New York Times

Life in the Minors

Nothing brings meaning to life more than having its experiences, what better way to chronicle the history of the Phillies Minor leagues than to speak with and record thoughts from some of those who've participated or continue to be a part of the climb. This chapter is entitled Life in the Minors and is a recollection of personal memories. We truly appreciate the following individuals who've shared recollections of their journey with us, it truly personalizes the Phillies Minor League history.

Gene Mauch, Dick Allen, Hank Allen & Ron Allen – Photo courtesy of Larry Shenk

Dick Allen

Within an hour after graduating from Wampum (PA) High School in 1960, Phillies scout John Ogden signed 18-year-old Dick Allen to a pro contract that included a $70,000 signing bonus. In April of that year, Ogden signed Dick's older brother Hank. In 1964, Ron Allen, the youngest brother, was signed by the Phillies.

Hank Allen reported to the Elmira Pioneers (Class D New York-Penn League). Dick joined the club in Geneva.

Playing in 88 games for the Pioneers, Dick had 19 doubles, 10 triples, 8 homers, 42 RB,I and a .281 average. Led club with .868 OPS.

19

Dick's Memories

"Jack Phillips was our manager, his first year. I wore number 5; played shortstop. Hank was the first baseman. Coy, my oldest brother, rented a house at 157 Light Street. Hank, me, and Bobby Sanders (infielder) lived there. Coy also bought a car for us to get around. Mom (Era) would come to see us when we played in Erie which was the nearest town to Wampum. What I remember most was getting hit in my left eye by a pitch and missing several weeks."

Hank's Memories

"What he didn't mention is he hit a home run in his first at-bat in pro ball that night in Geneva. I remember him getting hit by the pitch. I was on deck. It was loud like it hit his bat but Dick was lying on the ground face down. He didn't move. Jack and I rushed to home plate and I lost it when I saw the blood. I still had my bat and I charged the mound. The pitcher, I don't remember his name, started running. I tossed the bat, chased him but I never got him.

"It was the second game of a doubleheader against Wellsville at home. We crushed them in the first game and were doing the same thing in the second game. Sanders hadn't had a hit and told Dick, 'I'm bunting for a hit.' Dick said, 'If you do, so will I.' Sanders beat out a bunt and Dick fouled off the first pitch while trying to lay one down. The next one hit him. Sanders and Dick were playing pro ball for the first time. None of us were aware of the unwritten baseball rule that you don't bunt with a big lead.

"Dick was hospitalized in Elmira for two-three days before the Phillies flew him to Philadelphia to see their doctors. He was gone for a couple of weeks with a concussion before returning to Elmira. Coy and I met him at the airport. Coy said we're going to the ballpark for some batting practice. Coy was the pitcher, Dick the hitter and I shagged. Coy's first pitch was at Dick's head. I remember him saying, 'If you are going to be afraid of getting hit, if you're not going to be tough, Mom's got dinner for you back home. You and I will leave tonight.' Coy's next pitch was up and in again. From then on, Dick showed no fear. Back then, the tough survived. The first at-bat that night he crushed a line drive to left that was caught on an unbelievable play by the left fielder. Next at-bat, line drive double to left."

Teammates
Dick, Hank, and RHP Paul Brown were the only players from that team to reach the majors.

Big League Careers
Dick made his major league debut on 9/3/1963 after four years in the minors (88 doubles, 40 triples, 82 home runs, 342 RBI, .305); All-Star in each of last three seasons. Moved to a new position (3B) in 1964, became NL Rookie of the Year. Set four Phillies rookie records that still exist, runs (125), hits (201), total bases (352), slugging percentage (.557). Played for Phillies (1963-69, 1975-76), Cardinals, Dodgers, White Sox (1972 AL MVP), A's. 15 total seasons, 7 All-Star teams, 351 home runs, .292 average. Phillies retired his #15 in 2020.

Hank played 11 years in the minors and seven in the majors (Senators, Brewers, White Sox). On the same team with Dick in Elmira and the White Sox. Major league scout for 19 years after playing days were over.

Ron played nine seasons in the minors and 14 games in the majors with the 1972 Cardinals.

Basketball
All three played basketball at Wampum High School. Hank and Dick were on the1958 and 1960 state champions. As a freshman, Ron played in one game with his two older brothers. He went to Youngstown State University on a basketball scholarship before pro ball.

Photo Courtesy of Larry Anderson

Larry Andersen

Larry Andersen was drafted by the Cleveland Indians in the seventh round of the 1971 draft. Following graduation from Interlake High School in Bellevue, WA, the 18-year-old signed with Cleveland, receiving a $10,000 bonus. He started out with the Reno Silver Sox in the California League (1-0, 7 games) and spent August in Sarasota, FL, site of the Indians Gulf Coast League team (0-3, 4 games).

"Most baseball players travel the whole country from small towns to large cities. From Yuma, Arizona to Williamsport, Pennsylvania from Bellingham, Washington to Fort Myers,

Florida, and numerous cities in between. For me, that was certainly the case.

"I lived in six different cities in major-league baseball covering 17 years, 12 cities in the minor-league's spanning 9 1/2 seasons as well as two foreign lands over six winters. An iPhone with GPS would certainly have come in handy, but in a day when my baseball cards were still printed in black-and-white, the technology available was restricted to paper maps that can NEVER be folded back up the way they were when purchased. I felt like I should have been working for a moving company as much as my "home" changed.

"I was traded, released, loaned out, sent down, optioned out purchased and a free-agent six times. When you figure the buses, the flights, apartments, hotels and motels, small locker rooms including trailers, fast food restaurants and dive bars due to our $5.00 a day meal money allowance ... well, that's life in pro baseball.

"Then, there was my first spring training, 1972, Tucson, Arizona. I was one of many minor leaguers with the Indians. My uniform number was something like 112...I think. I was nervous and scared and, after one day, fighting blisters from the Kangaroo spikes. What did I like? Absolutely nothing. I grew up in Washington (State) so the warm weather was nice. But I couldn't handle the Arizona heat. I really struggled, especially all that running.

"Highlight of my minor league career was being the 'ace' on the 1976 Williamsport Tomahawks. I was 9-6 on the worst team in the Eastern League (48-91). Oh, I also led the team in hitting, .500 (1-2) plus a walk."

Teammates
Seven players from the 1971 Reno Silver Sox played in the majors. "LA" and C Alan Ashby had the longest careers, 17 seasons each.

Big League Career
Originally a starter, LA wound up as a reliever in the majors, 40-39, 49 saves, 3.15 ERA for 699 games (1 start). He pitched for the Indians, Mariners, Phillies (1983-86), Astros, Red Sox, Padres, and Phillies (1993-94). Pitched in 1983 and 1993 World Series for Phillies. Following his playing career, he was a pitching coach at Reading (1995-96) and Scranton/Wilkes-Barre (1997). Has been a member of the Phillies broadcasting team since 1998.

Photo courtesy of Mike Schmidt

Mike Schmidt

Following graduation from Fairview High School in Dayton, OH, Mike Schmidt headed for Ohio University where he led the Bobcats to the 1970 College World Series. A shortstop, he was drafted in the second round (30th overall in the draft; George Brett was 29th) in 1971. Schmidt was signed by Phillies scout Tony Lucadello who had followed him since he played Little League ball.

Mike was sent to the double-A Reading Phillies six days after he signed (June 11). In 74 games, he hit .211, 8 homers and 31 RBI. He was the shortstop the entire season. For 52 games, Bob Boone played next to Mike at third base.

"After I signed, I was asked to play in an exhibition game for the Phillies in Reading against the Reading Phillies because Larry Bowa was sick. Yes, all about timing. I hit a late-inning home run to win the game off of a Reading pitcher named Mike Fremuth, who had been acquired a few days earlier from Detroit for Tony Taylor. That home run probably saved me a year in my career.

"Yes, unusual. I was scheduled for Peninsula, their high-class A team, because I had come from a very highly respected college program. Placing me in Reading put me in a league that was a bit strong for my ability as a hitter at that time, but in my case, they decided to let me take my lumps and figure it out. Starting out in AA in the middle of the season was difficult.

"That was the first time I had been out in the world to fend for myself. I stayed in a hotel, I think the Ben Franklin or Abe Lincoln, in downtown Reading. It was old, a bit rundown, and I moved outside the city to the Reading Motor Inn which was closer to the stadium. There weren't a lot of fond memories in Reading, outside of playing golf in the area.

"The next year I moved up to AAA in Eugene. I started at third and a month into the season John Vukovich and I switched positions and I went to second, which helped both of us get on track.

"In 2004, after Donna and I agreed to my pursuit of a major league managerial job, I became the manager in Clearwater. That was some experience. We didn't have a very good team, mostly transplanted players on their way out, maybe a couple of prospects. My job was not to win games, it was to develop talent, something that I understood, but didn't feel it would further my cause pursuing my goal. I did my best to do both.

"As luck old have it the major league job came open at the end of the season. Ed Wade, then GM, opted not to grant me an interview. He hired Charlie Manuel, end of story."

Teammates
Mike was one of 13 on the Reading Phillies to reach the majors. Most prominent, in addition to Schmidt were Bob Boone and Andre Thornton.

Big League Career
A journey that began in Reading ended in Cooperstown, NY, one of 52 Hall of Famers to spend an entire career with one team. Acclaimed as the greatest player in Phillies history, Schmidt compiled numbers that are unmatched: 3 NL MVP Awards, 1980 World Series MVP, 8-time NL home run leader, 548 homers (7th all-time when he retired), 10 Gold Gloves, 12 All-Star teams (9 as a starter), 6 Silver Slugger Awards. Held 14 major league records, 18 NL records, 24 Phillies career records, and 11 Phillies season records when he retired in 1989. 18 years in a Phillies uniform is yet another record.

Photo courtesy of Larry Bowa

Larry Bowa

Baseball's first summer draft was 1965. A total of 824 players were selected. Larry Bowa, a skinny shortstop from Sacramento, CA, who just graduated from McClatchy High School wasn't among them. Phillies signed him that fall, a $1,200 signing bonus. Went to first spring training in 1966 in Leesburg, FL. Assigned to Spartanburg in the Class A Western Carolinas League.

Memories

"I was ready to quit after my first game, 0-4 with 4 strikeouts against this young fireballer, Nolan Ryan. Told the manager (Bob Wellman), 'Better get me a plane ticket home.' Bob talked me out of it. Four of us rented a house. Tommy Silicato, Barry Lersch; can't remember the fourth. Wore old uniforms, hand-me-downs from the Phillies. Those flannel uniforms were hot and hot it was in Spartanburg. Depending on the heat, we would work out in the morning of home games. Nothing but fundamentals. Ate a lot of burgers. We had no overnight road trips. Bused there, played the game, bused home.

"That season was probably the most fun I had in the minor leagues. We had an unbelievable season, 91-35; league champions. Won 25 in a row in July-August. That's almost a month without losing a game. In that streak, we had 20 complete games. We led the league in runs, hits, doubles, average, ERA, complete games, and shutouts but were last in home runs and strikeouts. Pat Williams was the GM and he had a promotion every night that filled the park. Trainer was Red Zipeta who also washed the uniforms. One day he was rubbing the right arm of one of the pitchers, Gordon Knutson. After a while, Gordon said, "That feels good but I'm lefthanded.""

A right-handed hitter then, Bowa wound up hitting .312 and striking out only 40 more times in 93 games. He finished the season playing five games in AAA at San Diego. Ironically, 21 years later he was the big-league manager of the San Diego Padres.

Teammates
Big leaguers from that squad included 1B Ron Allen, 2B Denny Doyle, RHP Barry Lersch, RHP Lowell Palmer, RHP Mike Strahler. OF Mel Roberts became a Phillies coach.

Big League Career
Major league debut, April 7, 1970, at Connie Mack Stadium against the Cubs. Hitless in 3 at-bats against Ferguson Jenkins, another future Hall of Famer. First MLB at-bat: pop up to short. Despite hitting .191 through the first two months, manager Frank Lucchesi stuck with him. Bowa

finished the season with a .250 average. Ended up with 2,191 hits in 2,247 career games and a .260 average. As a shortstop, he was automatic, only 211 errors in 19,058.1 innings. Four-time All-Star, 3 Gold Glove Awards. As a player, coach, manager coach, he's worn a Phillies uniform longer than anyone in Phillies history.

Photo courtesy of the Phillies

Bobby Wine

Bobby Wine was a much sought-after shortstop his senior year (1957) at Northport High School on Long Island. Phillies scout Dale Jones signed him. "After graduation, we went to Philadelphia on the train, met [Phillies owner] Mr. Carpenter and I signed. Got $4,000. When I got home, the Yankees, Reds and Red Sox came calling, but I said, 'Sorry, I signed with the Phillies.'"

His first pro season was that summer in Johnson City (TN) in the short-season (72 games) Class D Appalachian League. His manager was Ben Taylor.

"Took a train from New York to Johnson City. My instructions were to go to a hotel, can't remember the name, and the ballpark the next day. When I got to the park, I was told I needed to buy a sweatshirt, t-shirt, sanitary socks, jockstrap, and a cup. Didn't know a thing about a jockstrap or cup or sanitary socks.

"After two days at the hotel, I was told I need to find a room. Bob Gontkosky, one of my teammates, said a bunch of guys had rented a house and I could join them. There were 10 of us in the house. I started by sleeping in a screened-in porch. Later, when a couple of the players got released or promoted, I got my own bedroom.

"We wore hand-me-down uniforms from the Phillies, those heavy, hot wool ones. Learned you had to get to the park early and scramble through a pile of pants to find a pair that fit. I weighed 160 pounds and most pants were too big.

"Every afternoon, when he had home games, we'd go to a movie, grab a burger from a little greasy-spoon joint, walk to the park, play a game, and walk back to the house. We rode a rickety-old bus for road games. Stayed in small hotels and got $1.50 per day for meal money. Kingsport wasn't too far away so we would bus there in the afternoon and back after the games.

"Looking back, it all seems so bizarre. But I was young then and having fun."

Wine played in 54 games and led the club in hitting (.337), run (53), doubles (11) triples (6), and RBI (42). His six home runs were second. Leading pitcher was Chris Short, 9-2, for

15 games (12 starts). "Wine-o" and "Shorty" were the only players on that team that reached the major leagues.

Wine spent 15 years in the majors, Phillies (1960; 1962-68) and (Expos, 1969-72). His career average is .215. "Yea, but I hit 30 home runs, one more than (Richie) Ashburn," he said laughing. Won a 1963 Gold Glove Award. Coached in the majors for the Phillies (1972-83), Braves (1985-92), and Mets (1993-96). Returned to the Braves as the advance scout under manager Bobby Cox. When Cox retired, so did Bobby. Resides in Norristown, PA, in a home he purchased from Tommy Lasorda.

Photo courtesy of the Phillies

Rick Wise

Rick Wise was a Madison High School phenom in Portland, OR, who was signed by Phillies scout Glenn Elliott on June 16, 1963, after leading his team to its first state championship. Signing bonus, $12,000. This was two years before the summer draft began. He then headed for the Bakersfield Bears in the Class A California League to begin his professional career.

The 17-year-old finished his first season, 6-3 with a 2.63 ERA for 12 games (9 starts). He struck out 98 in 65 innings while walking only 23. Made his major league debut, April 18, 1964.

Memories
"Bob Wellman was the manager, "Bear" was his nickname. He was a huge man but easygoing. Made you feel at ease right from the start. We stayed in a hotel, roommate was Sammy Martinez, another pitcher. We had a midnight curfew which he often broke."

"Don't remember my first game but recall a three-game winning streak. Two were two-hitters and in the third, I struck out 12."

"Learned quickly that minor league life included a lot of bus rides. What I remember the most was the heat. It was hot all the time. Being from Oregon I wasn't used to it. I remember Sunday doubleheaders. The sun set over the batter's eye in center field. Tough for batters and fans to see. More than once, the second game didn't start until the sun went down."

Teammates
Players from that club who made it to the majors included outfielder Johnny Briggs and six pitchers, Rich Beck, Dave Bennett, Grant Jackson, Darrell Sutherland, Gary Wagner, and Bill Wilson.

Career
Wise went on to an 18-year career in the majors with the Phillies, Cardinals, Red Sox, Indians, and Padres. Final record: 188-181, 3.69 ERA for 506 games (455 starts).

His first start in the majors came as an 18-year-old, second game of a doubleheader in Shea Stadium, June 21, 1964, after Jim Bunning had pitched a perfect game vs. the Mets in the first game . . . Only pitcher in major league history to hit two home runs while pitching a no-hitter, Phillies 4-0 win in Cincinnati, June 23, 1971. On September 18 of that season, he set a Phillies record by retiring 32 consecutive Cubs in a 4-3, 12-inning win at Connie Mack Stadium. He singled in the winning run.

As a 12-year-old, pitched in the Little League World Series. Three years later he pitched the second no-hitter in Babe Ruth League World Series history. Most wins in the majors came with the 1975 Red Sox (19-12). Winning pitcher in Game 6 of the 1975 World Series.

Photo courtesy of the Phillies

Juan Samuel

His first start in the majors came as an 18-year-old, second game of a doubleheader in Shea Stadium, June 21, 1964, after Jim Bunning had pitched a perfect game vs. the Mets in the first game . . . Only pitcher in major league history to hit two home runs while pitching a no-hitter, Phillies 4-0 win in Cincinnati, June 23, 1971. On September 18 of that season, he set a Phillies record by retiring 32 consecutive Cubs in a 4-3, 12-inning win at Connie Mack Stadium. He singled in the wining run.

Juan Samuel was signed by the Phillies Kiki Acevedo and Ruben Amaro Sr. on April 29, 1980, out of the Dominican Republic. Bonus was $2,500. His pro debut came that summer with the Bend (OR) Phillies in the Northwest League. Bend was some 5,700 miles from his home.

Memories
"Went to Clearwater but many of us actually trained in Sarasota at a complex shared by the Braves and Astros. I was a second baseman, but they kept working me out in right field. I wondered if they confused me with someone else. I remember sitting on the bench and crying. P.J. (Carey, Phillies minor league manager), came up to me and asked what was wrong. Told him I wanted a plane ticket so I could go home. He talked me out of it. He wound up as my manager in Bend. We became close friends. He came to San Francisco when I played my first game in the majors.

"Later we joined extended spring training at the complex. I wasn't playing much and figured I would be sent back to the Dominican. I remember hitting a grand slam in a game and that sort of changed things.

"Walked in the complex clubhouse one morning and my name was on the list of players going to Helena. I was really surprised. The Phillies held a mini-camp there that included players they drafted. Darren (Daulton) was one I remember. He was assigned to Helena and I went to Bend.

"We stayed in a hotel. Four of us from the island hung together, Sergio Isambert, Alfredo Reynolds, and Juan Acevedo who was Nino Espinosa's brother. One day we noticed the American teammates checking out of the hotel.

37

One told me the club was only paying for a hotel room for one week. My buddies and I got a newspaper, checked out apartments, and found one. My mother was from St. Thomas so I knew some English. I was the interpreter. (Laughing).

"Out of the four of us, I was the only one to make it. Had a lot of fun that summer. Saw my first snow in Walla Walla. Lot of time riding buses. Longest trip was Victoria, Canada. We stopped a game one time on get-away day in the sixth inning. The bus had to get to the Canadian border by a certain time to catch the last ferry."

Samuel wound up playing 69 games and hitting .282. He showed the power (11 doubles, 17 home runs) and speed (26 steals) that would be his trademark in the majors. He walked 17 times and struck out 87 times. He later was quoted, "You don't walk off the Island. You Hit."

Teammates
Two others played in the big leagues, OF Jeff Stone and C Jerry Willard.

Big League Career
He wore a Phillies uniform for seven seasons (1983-89), hitting .263, and seven years as a coach (2011-2017). Set Phillies rookie records in 1984 for at-bats (701), triples (19) and stolen bases (72). In 1987, Samuel became the first player in major league history to reach double figures in doubles, triples, home runs and stolen bases in each of his first four major league seasons. Overall played 16 seasons in the majors, 287 doubles, 102 triples, 161 home runs, 396 stolen bases and a .259 average. He was a three-time All-Star.

Photo courtesy of the Phillies

Greg (The Bull) Luzinski

Upon graduation from Notre Dame High School (Niles, IL) in 1968, 17-year-old Greg Luzinski had a decision to make. He had big-time football scholarship offers (fullback/linebacker) and the Phillies made him their first-round selection in the summer draft, the 11th overall selection. "The Bull" chose baseball.

A catcher/first baseman, Luzinski reported to the Huron (SD) Phillies in the Northern League. His pro debut manager was Dallas Green, who was making his managerial debut and one of his teammates was a 17-year-old skinny catcher from Venezuela, Manny Trillo. Twelve years later the trio were World Champions.

Memories

"We had a mini camp for about a week. First time I met Dallas. He was loud and demanding a preview of things to come. His wife, Sylvia, was expecting so she stayed back east. Dallas spent a lot of time at the ballpark, drilling us on how to play the Phillies way. We did a lot of running, foul pole to foul pole, and then up and down the park's steps.

Dallas got tossed a few times. That hat of his took a beating. He'd throw it on the ground, kick it, you could see the dust fly.

"Lived with a host family, me, Roger Noble, and Allen Bowers. We lived in the basement. Living was free but we paid them because they did the laundry. The Plains Hotel was across the street from the ballpark. Ate there most of the time because we got a discount. Four of us chipped in to buy a used car to get back and forth to the park. We had the trunk removed and a couple seats put in. We'd pick up guys at different stops and were overloaded more often than not.

"There was a man-made lake, I guess that's what you would call it, not too far from the park. If we had a chance, we'd go swimming. Meal money for road trips was something like a buck a day.

"Remember one time it had been raining and the infield was pretty muddy. Went out to the dugout and there was this guy trying to help. They poured gas on the dirt, lit it, and then raked and raked. Learned he was Ruly Carpenter, son of the Phillies owner. That was my introduction to him. He was a great owner. Paul Owens would visit from time to time. Didn't know who he was either but learned.

"You know with Ruly, Pope, and Dallas the Phillies became a great organization. They were baseball people.

"I skipped Spartanburg the next year and went to Raleigh-Durham. We had drafted a guy named Bob Boone. He pitched and played third base at Stanford. He joined the club after the draft. I can still see him walking in the clubhouse wearing a Stanford jacket and carrying fishing rods. I introduced myself and asked him what he was going to do with the fishing gear. He said he hoped to go fishing once in a while. I told him there won't be any time. Better pile that stuff in your locker."

Luzinski played first base the entire season at Huron, hit .259 and, led the league with 13 home runs and 43 RBI which are Huron records. He spent four seasons in the minors and was an All-Star three of the seasons. Career minor league numbers: 113 home runs, 369 RBI, .303 average. Batting champion (.325) and Eastern League MVP in 1970.

Teammates
Four players on the Huron club made it to the majors. Luzinski, Trillo, catcher Larry Cox, and a reliever Dyar Miller.

Big League Career
Made his debut on September 9, 1970, wearing #42. Wound up playing 11 years with the Phillies (1970-1980) and four back home with the Chicago White Sox (1981-84). He and Mike Schmidt were the power bats in the middle of the Phillies lineup for nine seasons. Career numbers: 1,821 games, 344 doubles, 307 home runs, 1,128 RBI, and a .276 average. Noted for his upper deck "Bull Blasts" at Veterans Stadium. Four-time All-Star with the Phillies and runner-up to the NL MVP in 1975 and 1977. 1978 Roberto Clemente Award winner. Inducted into the Toyota Phillies Wall of Fame in 1998. Hosts Bull's BBQ ever since Citizens Bank Park opened in 2004.

Photo courtesy of Phillies

Larry Christenson

Following an outstanding senior year at Marysville (WA) High School, the Phillies selected Larry, right-handed pitcher, in the first round of the 1972 draft. He was the third overall selection on June 6. In 72 innings, he walked 12, struck out 143, and had a 0.28 ERA. Included was a no-hitter, five one-hitters, a .406 average, and four home runs. This came on the heels of starring on the basketball team that won the state championship.

Five days after the draft, he was signed by area scout Bill Harper and Brandy Davis, a scouting supervisor. His pro debut came with the Pulaski (VA) Phillies in the Appalachian Rookie League. In eight games (six starts) he posted a 4-2 record and 2.84 ERA; fanned 42 in 38 innings

Memories

"I signed the day after graduation. My family, girlfriend, and I were flown to Philadelphia a couple of days later. Got to work out at Veterans Stadium. Met Steve Carlton. A few days later my family returned home and I was driven to Pulaski by Wally Moses, an elderly gentleman. I had no idea who he was but learned he was the Phillies' roving minor league hitting instructor and a pretty darn good hitter in his time. It was a long ride with little conversation. I slept most of the afternoon.

"Roomed with Rocky Skalisky, another pitcher, in a boarding house owned by Mrs. Martin. We had a bedroom on the second floor. Remember putting a six-pack of beer in the refrigerator one day. It was gone the next day. Mrs. Martin didn't allow beer.

"I wore a hand-me-down #14 Jim Bunning uniform. Again, had no idea who he was. Two years later he was my triple-A manager in Toledo. My first manager was Harry Lloyd. We had a few workouts before the season began. A bunch of instructors were there, Granny Hamner, Larry Rojas, Lou Kahn, and Bob Tiefenauer.

"We played a doubleheader on opening day. I started the second game, pitched a complete game (7-innings). Didn't remember the details until I got out a scrapbook. Gave up two runs on four hits, walked nobody, and struck out 11. My first at bat I hit a home run. The newspaper clipping said it was hit to right. That's wrong. It was to center.

"Road trips were long and in an old, beat-up bus. I'll never forget the trip to Bluefield, WV. We pulled up to the hotel but our two black players weren't allowed in the hotel. They had to sleep on the bus. I couldn't believe it. I had no idea such discrimination existed.

"Bunky Warren was the pitching coach. He wanted to change my delivery after my second start. I wound up hurting my back and he was fired. Tiefenauer, the roving pitching coach, replaced him. I could throw the fastest, wildest knuckleball but the organization didn't want me to throw it."

Teammates
"LC" was the only player on the team to reach the show.

Major League Career
Went to his first spring training the next season (1973) and made the Phillies opening day roster. Made his debut on Friday, April 13 and beat the Mets, 7-1, before 7,127 at Veterans Stadium. Allowed five hits, walked six, struck out three, picked a runner off first in his complete game victory. Struck out the first hitter, SS Bud Harrelson. Wore #38 his entire 11 seasons with the Phillies, longest tenure for anyone playing his entire Phillies career wearing the same number. Finished career with 83-71 record, 3.79 ERA for 243 games (220 starts); 1-2 for 6 postseason games. Best season was 1977, 19-6. Shares club record with Rick Wise for most career home runs by a pitcher, 11.

Jimmy Rollins

Photo courtesy of Best Baseball Card Co.

Jimmy Rollins

Scouting Report

"This youngster can pick and throw. He has range, quickness, supple hands, strong/accurate arm. Excellent instincts and field smarts. Switch hitter; swing is compact with short stride, makes sharp contact from both sides. Tool wise, it's all there, except power, but it comes in a small package. Will be an early pick by a club that will go for tools over size. He CAN play and he can play shortstop in the major leagues," Phillies scout Bob Poole, March 1996.

The Phillies selected Jimmy in the second round of the 1996 draft, 46th overall player chosen, following an outstanding career at Encinal High School in Alameda, CA. "J-Roll" finished his high school career as holder of 10 records, including highest average (.484) and most stolen bases (99). Had a baseball scholarship to Arizona State University but chose pro baseball.

Went right to the Martinsville (VA) Phillies in the Appalachian Rookie League. Manager: Ramon Henderson. Wound up playing 49 games (all at shortstop). Hit .238, 1 home run, 18 RBI, 11 stolen bases, 28 walks, 20 strikeouts, 20 errors. Next season he moved up to the Class A Piedmont Boll Weevils of the Class A South Atlantic League.

Martinsville Memories

"Had been out of California by playing traveling ball since I was 8 but my first time in Virginia. Wore #2, I think. I lived with a host family who lived about 300 feet behind the left field fence. Easy walk to the ballpark. Sometimes hopped over the fence. Had two roommates, Kris Stevens, a left-handed pitcher from my state who was the 3rd round pick and another pitcher but his name escapes me.

"Biggest difference between high school and pro ball was playing every day and no off days. Plus adjusting to the heat. Remember I grew up in northern California. Ramon gave some great speeches especially when we lost a few games in a row. We had a tough season (20-47)."

Teammates

Only J-Roll and RHP Carlos Silva climbed to the majors from that team. At 17, they were the youngest players.

Major League Career

Debut came at Veterans Stadium against the Nationals, September 17, 2000; 0-2 at-bat … Played 17 years in the big show, Phillies (2000-14), Dodgers (2015), White Sox (2016). Final numbers: 2,275 games, 2,455 hits, 511 doubles, 115 triples, 231 home runs, 936 RBI, 470 stolen bases, .264 average … Table-setter for 5 division titles, 2 pennant winners and 2008 World Champions ... 3-time NL All-Star, 2007 NL MVP, 4 Gold Gloves, 2007 Silver Slugger Award, co-Roberto Clemente Award (2014) . . . Phillies Record Book: #1 hits (2,306), doubles (479), at-bats (2,306) ... #2 games (2,090), extra-base hits (806), total bases (3,655), stolen bases (453) ... #3 runs (1,325), singles (1,500), triples (111) ... #6 RBI (887) ... #9 home runs (216, most for switch-hitter) ... shortstop: most home runs (214, career); HR season (30, 2007), triples, season (20, 2007), RBI, season (94, 2007) ... most home runs, leadoff hitter (46) ... longest hitting streak (38 games, 2005-06) and longest single season streak (36 games, 2005).

Photo courtesy of Mickey Morandini

Mickey Morandini

A shortstop at Indiana University, Mickey Morandini took an unusual route to playing in the big leagues with the Phillies. He was originally a seventh-round selection of the Pirates in 1987. He didn't sign and was picked in the fifth round by the Phillies the following year. But he never put on a Phillies uniform until spring training of 1989. In between, he won a Gold Medal as a member of Team USA in the Olympics held in Seoul, Korea, in September of 1988.

His pro debut season wasn't the norm as he played in three different levels. Following spring training at Carpenter Complex, he was assigned to the Spartanburg Phillies. After 63 games (.338) he moved up to the Clearwater Phillies (17 games, .302) and then the AA Reading Phillies (48 games, .351). Combined .338 in 128 games. In 1990, he played at Scranton/Wilkes-Barre before making his major league debut on September 1 of that season.

Memories

"Mel Roberts was my Spartanburg manager and I wore number 5, my college number. Went 2-for-4 in my first game. First hit was a blooper to left field. Roomed in an apartment with Todd Elam. He had a car which was a bonus. Very excited that I got my first pro baseball card only to see my first name was listed as Mike.

"Elam was promoted to Clearwater and I soon followed. Roommate with a car again. Kim Batiste was the shortstop but he was moved to third base while I played short. I was only there for a couple of weeks before being moved up to Reading. Was able to get my own car from Indiana.

"Road trips were different at each level. Spartanburg had mostly long trips, Clearwater few overnights, and Reading had a mixture. Accommodations for road trips in college were better."

Teammates
Playing for three different teams Mickey had a lot of teammates, many of whom reached the majors. Most prominent, RHP Andy Ashby (Spartanburg/Clearwater), Batiste (Clearwater), Steve Scarsone (Clearwater/Reading), and LHP Chuck McElroy (Reading).

Major League Career
Spent 11 years in the majors, Phillies (1990-97, 2000), Cubs (1998-99), and Blue Jays (2000). Played in 965 Phillies games, finished with 911 hits and a .267 average. Member of 1993 NL champion Phillies and 1995 NL All-Star team. 1989 Paul Owens Award winner. After pro ball, coached Valparaiso (IN) High School baseball team for four years (2007-10). Returned to the Phillies as a minor league coach (2014-15, Lehigh Valley, Reading). Thereafter, minor league manager at Williamsport (2011) and Lakewood (2012-13) and big-league

coach, first base and base running (2016-17). Club Ambassador since 2018.

Photo by Miles Kennedy

Charlie Manuel

A four-sport star athlete (basketball, baseball, football, track and field) at Parry McCluer High School in Buena Vista, VA, Charlie Manuel received college basketball offers and was pursued by several major league teams. He chose baseball signing with the Minnesota Twins following graduation in 1963. Signing bonus: $20,000.

The Twins sent the 19-year-old to Wytheville, VA, their rookie club in the Appalachian League. In 58 games, he hit 7 homers, drove in 45 runs, and finished fourth in the league in hitting, .358. No record of his swing path, launch angle, or bat speed.

Memories

"I actually went to first and second grades in Wytheville. My dad was a Pentecostal evangelist in that area at the time.

"My aunt lived in Wytheville, so I lived with her during my first pro season. She drove me to the ballpark and took good care of me. Red Norwood was the manager. Another red head Virginian, Harrisonburg. I remember my number, 9...Ted Williams you know.

"We worked out for a week-10 days before the season started. We had something like 50-52 players. Some went to other Twins minor league teams and I saw some get released. That was a first … (laughing) … years later I was the guy releasing players. I was signed as a pitcher but hit some out of the park in squad games. Sherry Robinson, the Twins farm director, was there. He came up to me and said, 'Grab your glove and go to right field.' That's where I spent most of my career, in the outfield, some at first base, and pinch hitting.

"First game, I hit an opposite field home run just inside the left field foul pole. Hit off Roger Nelson of the Middlesboro Cubsox at home.

"When we played a road game, we got 50 cents as meal money. That could buy a hot dog or burger. When we had overnight trips, we got a raise, $1.50. Hotels were new to me, just the start of hundreds in my career if you know what I mean.

"I remember playing the Bluefield Orioles one time. Billy Hunter was their manager. He came up to me at the cage, 'Son, what cornfield did you walk out of?''

Teammate
Only one other player from that team climbed the ladder to the major leagues, outfielder Reggie Smith.

Minor League Manager
Following his playing career, Charlie returned to the minor leagues as a manager of the Wisconsin Rapids (WI) Twins in the Midwest League in 1983. He had played there in 1967.

"When you are in the low minors, you do everything. I had no coach. I'd be the first one at the park and last one to leave. I dragged the infield, lined the batter's box/foul lines, helped put the tarp on, mowed the grass.

"We had a Sunday game where I went to the mound to take out the pitcher. He complained that there was something wrong, the mound and home plate didn't seem lined up. Wasn't sure what he was talking about. Next morning, I went out with some nails, measuring tape, and a ball of twine, ran the twine from home plate to the pitcher's mound. Found out the rubber was 18 inches closer to home plate than it should be.

"We had a terrible start like 9-27. The second half we got a good hitter, Jeff Trout, a fifth-round third baseman out of the University of Delaware...yeah, Mike's dad. We got rolling and went into Appleton, a half-game out of first. Won the first game to move into first place for the first time. Lost the next two. The first loss was to a right-hander, Steve Noworyta."

Overall Career
Spent 11 seasons as a player in nine different minor league cities . . . Played against the likes pf Greg Luzinski, John

Vukovich, Larry Andersen, Mike Schmidt, Larry Christenson . . . Played six years in the majors with the Twins and Los Angeles Dodgers . . . Six years in Japan (1976-81); 1980 with Kintetsu Buffaloes (photo) was best season: 48 homers, 129 RBI, .325 . . . Managed nine years in the minors and 12 years in the majors, including nine with the Phillies (2005-13); winningest manager in Phillies history; World Champion in 2008 . . . Has also scouted, been a minor league roving hitting instructor, major league hitting coach and interim hitting coach (2019 Phillies) . . . Special Assistant to Phillies GM Ed Wade (2003) and Senior Advisor (since 2014).

Job Description of a Senior Advisor?
"Talk hitting in spring training with big club and minors, do some scouting of high school and college ballplayers for the draft, pal with Larry Bowa in visiting our minor league teams during the summer, stop by Citizens Bank Park to watch the big club. Hey, I'm a baseball lifer...I belong at the ballpark."

Photo courtesy of the Phillies

Bob Boone

As a pitcher at Crawford High School in San Diego, Bob Boone was undefeated as a pitcher, 27-0. He went to Stanford University where he pitched and played third base. Led team in wins (9-1) and hitting (.311) his last year. The Phillies drafted him in the sixth round in 1969, 126th overall player. Bob went right to Class A ball with the Raleigh-Durham Phillies in the Carolina League. In 80 games, he hit .300. Started at third base in 79 games.

Memories

"After I signed, Eddie Bockman (Phillies scout) said I was going to Raleigh-Durham. Bret had just been born and was going to be baptized so I asked if I could report a few days later. Sue and I were living in San Diego and the Phillies were in town that weekend. I worked out with the big club for a couple of days. Bockman said someone would meet me at the Raleigh airport. But when I got there, no one was there. So, I took a cab to the Raleigh ballpark, but the game was being played in Durham. So, I went to a bus terminal and took a bus to the Durham ballpark. I quickly learned there were two home parks.

"When I finally got to Durham it was the middle of the game. I sat in the stands with the GM, don't remember his name. I do remember him pointing out the first baseman, a kid named Greg Luzinski. GM said he's only 18 years old. I took one look and thought he's too big for that age. Greg and I hit it off, the beginning of a life-long friendship that includes our wives and kids.

"Nolan Campbell was the manager and said they wanted to ease me into playing. Heck, I was hungry to start right away. So, I'm in the lineup for the first time, a road game but don't remember the town. A bank of lights was out and the game was postponed. That was my welcome to pro ball. I quickly got on a hot streak, reached base for something like 14 straight at-bats, hitting .400. I hit some balls hard, got a couple of flairs, and reached base on an error. I was rolling. Elmer Valo, the Phillies minor league hitting instructor, came to town. He wanted to change my approach to produce more power. First game, pitches were by me before I could get my swing started. Said to myself, this isn't going to work but I'll give it another try. Second game, same story. I then decided I'm going to go back to my old approach.

"At Stanford, we flew to road games. Now, bus rides. Guys car-pooled to Durham from Raleigh for games. Those with cars got $3.00 for driving. I don't remember the meal money for road trips, but it wasn't much. We had first-class uniforms at Stanford. At Raleigh, hand-me-downs. My pants were so worn and thin you could see my legs.

"At Stanford, I played third base and pitched. But I wanted to play third base. When the Phillies drafted me, I asked Bockman if I was drafted as a third baseman or pitcher. He said third base. If he had said pitcher, I don't believe I would have signed. Medical school was in the picture.

"After that first season, I was sent to the Florida Instructional League in Clearwater. Twenty of us in that group made it to the majors. I was back at the FIL again after the 1970 season. Paul Owens wanted to move me from third base to catcher. I was leery about it. I thought I could play third in the majors and felt catching was a demotion. I went back to Reading, played mostly at third base with 30-some games behind the plate. In 1972, I went to triple-A in Eugene. Andy Seminick was the manager and my catching mentor. I caught 133 games, was called up to the majors on September 10.

"I hit one home run that September and so did Mike Schmidt. What people don't realize I was tied with Mike in career home runs until the following April. He zoomed by me."

Teammates
Eight players on the R-D team wound up playing in the majors. Longest careers, however, were Boone and Luzinski.

Career
Played 19 years in the majors with Phillies, Angels, Royals. Caught 2,225 games, third most all-time . . . Seven Gold Gloves, four-time All-Star . . . Managed two years in triple-A for A's and the Royals and Reds, three seasons each, in the majors . . . Has been a member of the Nationals front office since 2005; currently an Assistant GM and Vice President,

Player Development . . . Phillies Wall of Fame inductee in 2005.

Family Affair

Bob's dad, Ray, played in the majors as did two of Bob's sons, Bret and Aaron. Combined the four played 6,569 regular season games in the majors. A third son, Matt, played seven seasons in the minors and a brother, Rod, four years in the minors and also at Stanford. A grandson, Jake, played at Princeton University and was drafted by the Nationals.

Photo courtesy of the Phillies

Dickie Noles

Dickie Noles was a Phillies fourth-round selection in 1975 out of Harding High School, Charlotte, NC. "Wes Livengood (Phillies scout) met me, my dad and high school coach at Denny's restaurant where I signed. Got a $28,500 bonus," he recalled.

Dickie went right from Charlotte to Auburn, NY, where the Phillies had a team in the New York-Penn League. His Auburn Phillies uniform was #8. His manager, June Raines. A starting pitcher, 18-year-old Noles pitched in nine games and finished with a 2-2 record.

Memories
"Spent first night in a motel and then moved into a guest home with three teammates. We were a little noisy for the other guests so Sammye Welborn (RHP) and I found a third-floor bedroom in another house. We had a kitchenette and our own outside entrance. Met my first Hispanic person, Orlando Isales (15-year-old OF from Puerto Rico). We became good friends throughout the minors.

"My fondest memory from that season was meeting Dallas Green (Director, minor leagues/scouting), Larry Rojas (minor league instructor), Bob Tiefenauer (roving minor league pitching coach). Each became an important part of my life, just not baseball.

"My most memorable moment on the field came in a game in which I gave up back-to-back homers. Believe they were the only two homers off me. Up until then, I had allowed one in Little League and one in high school. After the first one, I thought I needed to throw harder. After the second one, I really overthrew so much so that "Tief" came out to the mound to try and calm me. I've never forgotten his final words, 'Get used to it. You're gonna give up a lot more.'

"Overall, there was nothing about that season that I didn't enjoy. It was the start of living a dream."

Teammates
Four players reached the major leagues, Isales, INF Jose Moreno, LHP Jeff Schneider, and Noles. Dickie was the only one with a career longer than three seasons.

Career
Spent 11 years in the big leagues. Debut was with the Phillies in 1979. First full season was 1980 when he was first converted into a relief pitcher. Remembered for knocking down George Brett in game 4 of the World Series that fall. In addition to four Phillies seasons, pitched for the Cubs, Rangers, Indians, Orioles, and Tigers. Final numbers: 36-53, 4.56 ERA, 277 games, 11 saves.

Photo courtesy Baseball Hall of Fame

Pat Gillick
Lawrence Patrick D. Gillick's baseball life is sprinkled with a College World Series championship, a minor league stint as a pitcher mirroring his father, an exceptional executive career

that includes three World Series rings, and an induction into the National Baseball Hall of Fame.

It all began at USC. In 1958, Pat was a bullpen piece on the Trojans who won the CWS although he didn't get in a CWS game. Late that summer, he signed a pro contract with the Baltimore Orioles, receiving a $4,000 bonus.

His pro debut came in 1959 with the Stockton Port, an Orioles affiliate in the Class C California League, not far from his Chico, CA, home. In 38 games (20 starts), the 21-year-old lefty was 9-5 with a 3.78 ERA. He walked 127 and struck out 127 in 162 innings.

Memories
"I had thoughts of going to law school following graduation. Played summer ball in Canada after which I was one of four the Orioles signed out of California. It was less expensive to fly four of us to spring training in Florida in '59 and then back to the coast so we trained with the Orioles AAA team in Yuma, AZ, and then reported to Stockton a few days before the season started.

"Billy DeMars was the manager. He was strict but likable. Taught us how to conduct ourselves as a pro, playing the game the right way.

"Pete Ward and I were roommates. We stayed in a hotel all season, $10 a night. Actually, had a suite. Rode our bikes to the park. Sometimes a teammate with a car would pick us up. I loved playing pro ball. I always had decent won/loss records and ERAs. My problem was control. I believe if I had better control and consistency I could have pitched in the majors.

"Pro ball really wasn't a major adjustment. Coach Rod Dedeaux ran the USC program like a pro team. We played games before our college schedule against AAA clubs that trained in the area, including some big-league teams.

"One game while at Stockton that I remember was against Visalia. Dave Bristol was their player-manager. I gave up a home run. Bristol was the next batter and I knocked him on his ass. After the next pitch, he threw the bat and charged the mound. My only fight in pro ball.

"My last season was 1963 in Elmira. Earl Weaver, the manager. I had some off and on injuries and couldn't solve control of the strike zone. So, I decided to give it up. I originally thought I would give it a try for five seasons. Law school was back in the picture. Paul Richards and Eddie Robinson headed player development with the Orioles. They both moved to the Houston Colt 45's expansion club in 1961. After I left baseball, Robinson called and offered a job as assistant farm director. His $3,900 salary offer wasn't appealing. Heck, I made $1,400 a month in triple-A. We talked and I got him up to $4,200.

"Looking back my career was intermingled with the Phillies. In every league I played, the Phillies had a team. Managers like Paul Owens, Andy Seminick, Frank Lucchesi. I played against guys like Pat Corrales, Lee Elia, Norm Gigon, Ray Culp, John Herrnstein, Dick Allen, Dennis Bennett, Danny Cater. Then when I was with Toronto, we trained in Dunedin just out the back door to Clearwater and the Phillies. I saw a lot of the same guys. DeMars was a coach, Owens the GM, Corrales a manager, Elia a coach. And, I was fortunate to end my career with the Phillies."

Teammates
LHP Bo Belinsky, INF-OF Pete Ward, RHP George Werley, C Frank Zupo all reached the majors from the 1959 Stockton club. So, did Gillick, but not on the mound.

Minor League Career
Five years, seven different teams (1959-63) . . . 43-28, 3.42 ERA record for 153 games . . . His father, Larry, was a right-handed minor league pitcher (1929-34); 42-48 for 163 games.

Executive Career
Gillick, 26, began a front-office career in 1963 with Houston where he was an assistant farm director, scout and scouting director. He moved to the New York Yankees in 1975, as a Coordinator of Player Development. In 1976, he joined the expansion Toronto Blue Jays as their Vice President of Player Personnel, and in 1977, their Vice President of Baseball Operations and General Manager. In 1984, he was named Executive Vice President of Baseball Operations. His Blue Jays won back-to-back World Series (1992-93).

He was also the GM of the Orioles (1996-98), Mariners (2000-2003), and Phillies (2006-2008) where he earned his third World Series ring in 2008. He remained with the Phillies (Sr. Advisor to the President/GM) and served as interim president (2014-15).

In 27 seasons as a general manager, his teams finished with 20 winning records. Each of his four teams advanced to the postseason, a grand total of 11 times.

Photo courtesy of Phillies

Kyle Kendrick

A three-sport star at Mount Vernon (WA) High School (football, baseball, basketball), right-handed pitcher Kyle Kendrick signed with the Phillies after he was selected in the seventh round in 2003. He turned down a football scholarship at Washington State University to play baseball.

After signing he was sent to Clearwater and the start of a professional career in the Gulf Coast League. He was 0-4 in nine games, five starts.

Memories

"Stayed in what was then the Econo Lodge next to Lenny's restaurant on Route 19. My roommate was Matt Linder, a pitcher from Canada. Phillies took him in the round after me. Every player in the GCL ate dinner every night at Lenny's, including Sundays which was a day off. Lunch was usually a sandwich at the Complex. We walked to and from the Complex six days a week.

"Ruben Amaro Sr. was our manager, very friendly but firm and very helpful. He had a sense of humor which was welcomed as we spent long hours at the Complex. Pitching coaches were Gorman Heimueller and Carlos Arroyo. I loved those guys. They were great mentors not only for pitching mechanics but the mental part of the game.

"Biggest adjustment was being away from home. I never left the state but now I was far away from home. I could throw hard but now everyone was the same. Some of the young Latin pitchers threw the hardest. As pitchers, we threw every day, something we didn't do in high school. We also worked daily at developing all your pitches. The heat didn't bother me. I adjusted to it and loved it. Easier to keep your arm loose.

"No overnight road trips, just bus rides to Lakeland, Tampa, Bradenton, Dunedin. We were notified the day before if we were going to be on the travel roster. Being a pitcher, you stayed back much of the time and worked out.

"My first game was a start against the Yankees on the Schmidt field. I struck out the first batter, Erick Almonte. He had been a back-up to Derek Jeter but on rehab assignment.

"Bummed a ride some nights to go see the Clearwater Phillies at Jack Russell Stadium. Ryan Howard, Cole Hamels, Ryan Madson, Carlos Ruiz, Gavin Floyd, Brandon Duckworth were on the club."

Teammates
Kendrick was one of three pitchers on the GCL roster that reached the majors, Scott Mathieson and Zack Segovia. Kyle had the longest career.

Major League Career
Kyle spent his first eight seasons in the majors in a Phillies uniform, posting double figures in wins six times, including 11-9 with the 2008 World Champions. Made his pro debut in June of 2007 and started game two in the NLDS that October, a loss. Also played one season in Colorado and very briefly with the Red Sox. Finished 81-83 with a 4.68 ERA in 255 games (214 starts). He also spent five full seasons in the minors.

Allen Greenwood

Allen Greenwood was a RHP in the Phillies organization for two seasons in 1969 and 1970. He's a Philadelphia area resident from Unionville, PA. While his time was brief as a professional baseball player his perspective on the experience mirrors that of many young players who've had the opportunity to play professionally yet didn't reach the ultimate goal of playing in the big leagues.

Memories

Greenwood was invited to an American Legion Baseball showcase game after his senior high school season. The showcase was in Northeast Philadelphia and he remembers going there with his legion coach. He was invited as a first baseman but his coach talked to the game manager and also got him a couple innings on the mound. Allen did well and a few scouts asked for his Legion game schedule to follow up.

His next legion game was in Downingtown and multiple scouts attended. He remembers that a few days later, two scouts from the Phillies, Joe Reilly and John Ogden (he also signed Dick Allen) came to his house and offered a contract which he signed. A few days later the eighteen-year-old was on his way to Pulaski, VA.

His manager at Pulaski was Dallas Green, in his second season as a minor league skipper. Greenwood remembers having great respect for Dallas, saying that he was welcoming but also a taskmaster, he expected the players to do their job.

Pulaski didn't have a dedicated pitching coach then, instead a roving coach would pass thru to the various cities. Bob Tiefenauer was the roving pitching coach when he first started, he had just concluded his ten-year major league career the year before. Individual coaching instruction was therefore limited to all pitchers in the system simply because there weren't team dedicated coaches. Allen remembers struggling to find control of his pitches and the lifestyle of being a pro player challenging. He shared a room with two other players, fast food were the meals they ate, and a different type of competition was introduced to him. As an amateur athlete his first priority was the team, as a pro it seemed to be more about competing against teammates for promotion instead of to simply trying to win games. It made him confused and, in his words, "I thought about it too much". He didn't find it enjoyable.

He didn't attend 1970 spring training; his contract had provided an allowance for college tuition so he was attending school when spring training occurred. Instead, his pro career resumed again in June with a return to Pulaski, albeit a short stay this time. In a couple of weeks, he was sent to Walla Walla, Washington to join the starting rotation of their staff. His manager there was Gary Powell. The roving pitching instructor was Ray Ripplemeyer who would later become the major league pitching coach for the Phillies.

Greenwood didn't fare much better in Walla Walla than in Pulaski on the field. He did enjoy the housing arrangement there better; it was a host family that took him in and the home-cooked meals he very much welcomed and appreciated.

Following the 1970 season he was released ... his minor league career consisted of a total of nineteen games. Allen said that he was relieved to be released, his youthful age, inexperience and the self-imposed pressure he put on himself made him press. He had developed a mental block, bad mechanics, and couldn't throw strikes. In his words, "It sounds self-deprecating but I wasn't a pitcher but rather a fastball thrower and had no idea how to pitch".

Allen was both homesick and had lost confidence in his playing ability. In retrospect, he considered it a blessing to have had the experience as it gave him the push to move on with other life pursuits. He returned to his hometown, started a successful business, and has been there ever since.

"There was a great deal of talent then that never ascended, it's not just on-field talent that matters, it's mental makeup as well, especially confidence and approach."

Greenwood places no blame on anyone other than himself for not being able to perform better as a pro, it was a life experience he will never forget, a true learning for a then naive young man from a small town south of Philly. He's never looked back with any despair and remains honored and humbled by the opportunity afforded him to play pro baseball.

Photo courtesy of Scott Palmer

Scott Palmer

Young ballplayers climb the ladder to the majors by honing their skills in minor league cities such as Jacksonville, Spartanburg, Asheville, and Birmingham. It's the same route Scott Palmer, the Phillies Director of Public Affairs, took as a young, aspiring journalism grad out of Western Illinois University back in the 1970s.

While in the U. S. Navy, Palmer was stationed in Jacksonville, FL, and worked as a studio cameraman at WLTV. When he was finished with active duty, he was hired as a reporter/anchor by WJKS TV, also in Jacksonville. In 1981, he reached the "majors" in Philadelphia as a sportscaster for WPVI TV. Along the way, he had stops in Spartanburg, SC (WSPA TV), Asheville, NC, (WLOS TV) and Birmingham, AL (WVTM TV). His "positions:" cameraman, sportscaster, news reporter, sports director, news anchor.

During his journey, Scott had two interesting minor league experiences, both involving the Spartanburg Phillies.

"While at WSPA TV, I went to Duncan Park to cover a Phillies game as a cameraman/reporter. I remember advice from my news director, 'When covering NASCAR, just film the crashes. Baseball, just the home runs.' Being an old, small park there were no positions for TV cameras and the press box was very small. So, I decided to go up on the roof. I'm filming the game and all of a sudden, I see a baseball coming my way. It was getting bigger and bigger. Before I could move, I got drilled in the solar plexus. Nobody was around, I was gasping for air while trying to hold onto the camera. Turns out I was alright, and the news director seemed to be more excited that we didn't lose a camera. I still have that ball as a painful souvenir."

His other baseball story was while he was at WLOS in Asheville, home of the Tourists, a minor league affiliate of the Rangers in the same league as the Spartanburg Phillies, Western Carolinas League. Wayne Terwilliger managed Asheville. The year, 1977.

"Our news director and the Tourists GM were friends. They came with a promotional idea of me doing a series on the life of a player in the minor leagues that would conclude with me playing in one game. I didn't want to embarrass myself, so I worked out with the team two-three times a week. When it came to the game, the Spartanburg Phillies were in town.

"I had to sign a pro baseball contract to be eligible to play. Got $1.00 and "other considerations", a hot dog after the game. I played right field and was told I would get two at-bats.

"Marty Bystrom was Spartanburg's pitcher. First pitch was a down-and-in fast ball called a strike. I heard it. I stepped out and suggested to the home plate umpire, 'That sounded a little low.' The ump snapped, 'Get back in there rook.' After hearing that fast ball, I figured I better be really quick with the bat. I got my bat on the next pitch, another fastball. I sliced it into the first base dugout. Next pitch was a curve ball which had me bending five different directions at once. Called strike three. When I got back to the dugout my teammates let me know, 'When you strike out you don't run back to the dugout. You walk and stare at the pitcher.'

"Second time up, I got the bunt sign. I was a pretty good bunter in high school, and I thought I might have a chance. First pitch, a high fastball that I popped up. Ozzie Virgil, the catcher, caught it. 0-for-2 in my career.

"I had one play in right field, a sinking liner that went off my glove for a double. Should have been a single and an error but I wasn't going to campaign for an error. After I was out of the lineup Terwilliger said, 'You can stay on the bench or go back to work in the studio.' I went to work."

One of Palmer's teammates was Dave Righetti who went on to a long career as a pitcher and pitching coach in the majors. They crossed paths in Philly when Righetti was with the Giants. While at WPVI Palmer covered the Phillies for years, including Bystrom and Virgil. Small world.

Palmer retired from WPVI in June of 2005. He quickly accepted an offer from Phillies president David Montgomery to join the front office as Director of Public Affairs. Scott's "positions": public relations, community relations, media relations, host a Sunday pre-game TV show "Beyond the Pinstripes" and interviews on phillies.com both during spring training and the season. When PA announcer Dan Baker was unable to work the 2020 season because of a health issue, Palmer pinch-hit.

Palmer's name can be found on baseball-reference.com because of his one-game minor league career. Just type his name, hit enter and it takes you to his page. For bats and throws the website lists "Unknown." To Philadelphians, he's well known.

Photo courtesy of the Phillies

Frank Coppenbarger
Like many kids, Frank Coppenbarger fell in love with baseball and worked his way up through the minors to the majors. Not as a player, but he did get to play one game in the minors while he was the clubhouse manager. For proof, go to baseball-reference.com and type his name. It will take you to "his" page. An incredible journey. Along the way, he connected with people who wound up with the Phillies during his career, first as clubhouse/equipment manager and later as director team travel (1989-2019).

That journey began in his hometown, Decatur IL, home to a minor league team (Commodores) of the Giants. "My parents worked so in the summer they would drop me off at my grandparents who lived close to the ballpark. Some evenings we'd walk by the park and even get a foul ball that was hit out of the park. Many times, I'd hang around the park and try to sneak in. I became a ballpark rat and bugged them so much they hired me as a bat boy. I was 11. My very first game was against Wisconsin Rapids Twins. We got beat. Some guy hit a grand slam ... Charlie Manuel," recalls Coppenbarger. Manuel, connection #1.

He learned an economics lesson very early. "One day the GM came up to me, 'Here's your money.' I told him no need to pay me. I love it. He gave me the money anyway. I learned to never say I don't need to be paid."

His first road trip came that summer to Burlington, IA. He roomed with Larry Unser, Decatur's clubhouse manager and younger brother of Del Unser.

Following high school graduation, Coppenbarger enrolled at Millikin University in his hometown. "Wanted to teach and coach." After a couple of years, he dropped out. Knew he really missed baseball. Dozens of letters to minor league and major league teams received negative responses, except one, the Quad Cities Angels (Davenport, IA), who offered him a job running the clubhouse in 1977. His first- full time job in baseball. "Chuck Cottier was the manager and he took me under his wing, a mentor on how to manage a clubhouse. Chuck also had me throw BP, hit fungos, shag, hit occasionally with pitchers, and take infield if they needed someone."

Cottier moved up to the Salinas (CA) Angels in the California League in 1978 and convinced the GM to bring 22-year-old Frank as the clubhouse manager. "Late in the season, Chuck asked me if I wanted to play in a game. I couldn't say yes fast enough. I signed a pro contract for $1.00—I still have the contract...not the dollar. I was the DH in the last game of the season against the Lodi Dodgers. Had one at-bat. Fouled off a couple of pitches and then the pitcher, a guy named Charlie Barrett, struck me out of a curve ball. Imagine throwing a curve ball against a "clubbie."

Coppenbarger batted third in the lineup and is quick to point out, Joe Maddon, a back-up catcher then, hit seventh. Maddon went on to become a major league coach and manager of the Rays, Cubs, and now Angels. Whenever their paths cross Frank always reminds Joe about that batting lineup.

Frank's journey as a clubbie carried him to Springfield (IL) where the Cardinals had their AAA affiliate in 1979. Hal Lanier was the manager. The Cardinals played an exhibition game in Springfield that season. Frank met Butch Yatkeman their clubhouse manager and expressed interest should a job open in St. Louis. Two years later Butch remembered and brought him to St. Louis as his assistant.

While at Springfield, Frank met Lee Thomas, first as the Cardinals traveling secretary before becoming the director of player development in 1980. Lee made numerous trips to

Springfield to watch the Cardinals, young players. When Thomas was named Phillies GM in 1988, he brought Frank to Philadelphia to manage the Phillies clubhouse.

Many young players participate in the fall instructional leagues early in their young careers. Check that off on Frank's resume. "I was the clubbie for the Angels in Mesa, AZ, for two years. Cottier and Jimy Williams were there as instructors. Jim Fregosi, the Angels manager, spent time there, too. My night job was to drive Fregosi and Cottier to restaurants and bars, you know, the designated driver. Once in a while did the same for Warren Spahn, then a pitching instructor."

Did Frank ever get close to playing in a major league game? "No," he responded quickly. "One time the Phillies were playing in Coors Field and I took some BP with the early guys. Did pepper a couple balls off the outfield walls. Little did I know Ed Wade (GM) was leaning on the cage. 'Frank. I've been looking for a left-handed bat for the bench. Didn't know I should look in the laundry room.'"

Yep, Frank Coppenbarger spent many late nights in empty ballparks washing uniforms. Tiny part of a clubbie's job description.

Photo by Michael Dill

Adam Haseley

OF ... HT: 6'1" WT: 190 ... Born: April 12, 1996, Orlando, FL ...
How Obtained: 1st round selection by Phillies in 2017 draft...
Attended the University of Virginia.

Adam made his major league debut with the Phillies on June
4th, 2019.

Memory of signing

"I went to play summer ball in the Cape and from the day I
got there until the night of the draft, all the 2017 eligible
draft guys were constantly being watched and evaluated.

I was notified about being selected in the draft a few
moments before it was announced on television. My agent
called me and said the Phillies were going to select me and
after we hung up, I was glued to the TV. Draft night was
definitely a surreal experience and something I'll remember
with my family and friends for a long time."

Pro debut

"To begin my pro career, I was assigned to the Gulf Coast League. After a few games, I was moved to Williamsport where I felt like I got my first taste of pro ball. My manager was Pat Borders and my hitting coach was Tyler Henson. Both helped me adjust to playing every day, which is the biggest difference between amateur ball and pro ball in my opinion."

Life as a pro

"In amateur ball, the most amount of games we would play in a week was four or five. In pro ball, we could go on stretches where we play up to twenty or more games in a row. Since we were on the field so much, I had to learn how to take care of myself off the field by eating, sleeping, and recovering better than I had before."

Photo by Michael Dill

Albertus Barber

RHP … HT: 6'2" WT: 175 … Born: February 18, 1996, Tulsa, OK … How Obtained: Amateur Free Agent signing 6/23/2019 … Attended Oklahoma Baptist University

Albertus has played in the GCL as well as Williamsport and Lakewood.

Memory of signing

"I remember being called in the 35th or 36th round by Zach Friedman. He was letting me know I had a possibility of being signed as a free agent. I remember watching every single pick on two phones, updating constantly, and in agony my name hadn't been called yet. It was awful. I hated every single bit of it until that phone rang and I was told there was a good chance I was going to be a Phillie. I had my background at CBP for two months prior to all of this and hoped I was going to be a Phillie. That was the only team I wanted/want to play for."

Pro debut
"I was nervous. I mean you look around and everyone is considered professional. You're competing for a spot on the 40-man one day but have to perform every day to get there. I remember Josh Bonifay sitting there staring at me, watching me warm up while my adrenaline was flowing and I sailed one to the backstop. I hadn't pitched in a game in over a year at this point, so my juices were flowing big time. The second I stepped on that field though my brain for the most part turned off. There was still nervousness and things I had to think about that I hadn't in a while since I hadn't pitched in a game, but for the most part it was back to my instincts."

Life as a pro
"People see you as a whole different person. You're now a larger-than-life character for some reason. While I think we are all just people, it's really cool being someone kids look up to. This is the most important part of being a pro. It's all about doing the most possible good you could do for others with that platform. You have an opportunity to change an unbelievable amount of lives. Really, the only differences to me are that I'm getting paid, the bats aren't metal, and everyone is a little bit bigger, but besides that, it's the same game."

Life in the minors
"I will always remember in my first year how different all of the cities and ballparks were. Some were small towns that five people would come to a game, but without that stadium, thirty people would be out of work. Then there're ballparks

with averages of thousands of people and the nicest facilities I've ever seen. It was so much different everywhere we went, but there was always baseball to be played and that's all that mattered. I stayed in Lakewood, New Jersey primarily, but we traveled all along the SAL league. I'll never forget how excited kids were to have their ball signed by a player. It didn't matter if you were the home team or the enemy, that kid's day was made. The fans are what make the game. We just play it."

Photo by Steve Potter

Ben Brown

RHP ... HT: 6'6" WT: 210 ... Born: September 9, 1999, East Setauket, NY ... How Obtained: 33rd round in 2017 draft ... Attended Ward Melville High School.

Ben has played in the GCL, at Williamsport and Lakewood ... he had Tommy John surgery in May of 2019 and is working his way back to action.

Memory of signing

"I found out I got drafted on Twitter, I just remember constantly refreshing the app after every pick and almost driving myself insane."

Pro debut

"I was assigned to the GCL and my manager was Roly de Armas. Showing up every day to a baseball field was a dream come true. In my first game, we were facing the GCL Braves and there were no more than ten people behind the backstop, but man did it feel packed. I had a couple really nice defensive plays behind me, thankfully, so I was able to get out of my first inning without letting up any runs."

Life as a pro

"The amount of preparation and time that goes into each start is much different than what I would do in high school. Playing all year compared to only six months out of the year Is also a pretty big difference."

Life in the minors

"I have been really lucky to have some time in the NYPL and the SAL and I know many people are not really a fan of long road trips but I really thought that whole experience of traveling up and down the east coast was so incredible. Rome (GA) was my favorite ballpark that I was able to play in so far."

Photo by Michael Dill

Darick Hall
1B/DH … HT: 6'4" WT: 232 … Born: July 25, 1995, Hereford, AZ … How Obtained: 14th round in 2016 draft … Attended Dallas Baptist University

Darick has played at Williamsport, Lakewood, Clearwater, and Reading. He received his first big league spring training invitation in 2020.

Memory of signing
"I remember getting a call on the third day of the draft notifying me that I was selected by the Phillies in the 14th round. My agent let me know and then the area scout, Paul Scott, called me to follow up. It was an amazing day and was a dream come true. I always had aspirations to become a professional but that was the reality of it."

Pro debut

"I was assigned to Williamsport shortly after the draft minicamp. My first manager was Pat Borders. Pat couldn't have been a better manager to have your first year. His knowledge of the game and his feel as a manager made him fun and easy to play for. His knowledge also benefitted each player that he had. I was very excited to start but after it hit me that I'd have to perform to keep my job and career going it made reality once again set in. Time to sink or swim.

I thought I was highly motivated to play in college but it seemed like it went up a notch in pro ball. I knew I always wanted to get to the big leagues and now was the time to do it."

Life as a pro

"Pro ball has also made me grow as a person and a man because it is a hard lifestyle. I love it but there are challenges that each person has to overcome. You become fully responsible for yourself and your career. That is a huge responsibility. You don't have people there all the time telling you what to do and you have to learn how to make decisions that will positively impact your performance because it matters."

Life in the minors

"The ballparks are always fun. You run into so many different environments, good stadiums, bad stadiums, tough crowds, no crowds, excited crowds. And, it's the same with cities. All the things we go through are to prepare us for the big leagues. At the lower levels, we had host families. But, as I progressed, we had to find our own spaces. In high A, I stayed in a house with seven guys and slept on an air mattress for example. All is worth it to get a chance to play in the big leagues. Once you make it, all the struggles you went through will be worth it."

Winning a League MVP Award (2017 - Lakewood)
"That team was such a joy to play on and it is really the same team I've played on since then. Our charisma and enthusiasm as a unit made it fun to be a part of. That team was full of a bunch of guys with great work ethics and the ability and willingness to grind. When everyone works hard you gain a ton of respect for your counterparts and it makes the environment good. What was most important was that we love winning and always want to win. That kind of culture is fun to play in."

Photo by Michael Dill

Jonathan Hennigan

LHP ... HT: 6'4" WT: 193 ... Born: August 27,1994, Nacogdoches, TX ... How Obtained: 21st round in 2016 draft ... Attended Texas State University

Jonathan has played at Williamsport, Lakewood, Clearwater, and Reading. He appeared in his first big league spring training game in 2020.

Memory of signing

"I got a phone call from my scout congratulating me on getting drafted. Crazy story. I received a phone call from the Boston Red Sox who were a few picks after the Phillies and verbally committed with them. Phone rings and it's the Phillies. Crazy stuff! "

Pro debut

"Williamsport was a little nerve-racking at first but it's a game. I try and keep every inning, every pitch like I have done it my whole life."

Life as a pro
"I would say the talent is the biggest difference, the hitters are disciplined. They hit the mistake a long way."

Life in the minors
"The ballparks at the lower level were a little lacking but the higher up you get the better they get. The fans are crazy! ... Very into the games."

Photo by Michael Dill

Will Hibbs
RHP ... HT: 6'7" WT: 245 ... Born: October 27, 1993, San Antonio, TX ... How Obtained: 19th round in 2016 draft ... Attended Lamar University

Will played at Williamsport, Lakewood, Clearwater, Reading, and Lehigh Valley. He retired from professional baseball after the 2018 season.

Memory of signing

"I heard my name called live at the start of the 19th round of the draft. I hadn't previously spoken with the Phillies, so I was surprised to hear my name. I remember going to play golf with my buddies the morning of the second draft day. We had just walked through the door coming back home when my friend said "alright well I'm ready to hear your name." No more than 30 seconds later, boom! Hilarious."

Pro debut

"I was first assigned to the Williamsport Crosscutters. Pat Borders was/is the manager there and is one of my favorites to this day. He does an exceptional job showing and explaining how pro ball differs from high school or college. He kept morale upbeat and light, which is important considering Williamsport is typically the first stop on the professional journey for players who otherwise have no professional experience and are nervous. In my first game I was so anxious I almost threw up. My first warm-up pitch went about 20 feet over the catcher. Funny thing is, I was completely calm and fine after that."

Life as a pro

"You have to have a selfish mindset about performing. The minor leagues are where "players develop, not teams. Obviously, everyone wants to win and help the team to the postseason, but no one ever said to themselves "I really dream about being the best single-A player ever to play the game." This sounds somewhat cynical, but it's the reality. This isn't to be confused with being a selfish teammate (that's a quick way to create bad blood throughout the organization)."

Life in the minors

"The cities are often small or secluded, making the baseball games a larger attraction for people living there. The things that stick in my mind most of all would have to be the various quirky promotions or traditions at each ballpark (the Toast Man, Star Wars Night, and the crowd favorite "10-cent Beer Night"). I stayed with host families in my Short-Season A and Low-A seasons. They are some of the nicest, selfless, and most caring people I've had the pleasure of meeting. We still keep in touch to this day - shout out to the Burch and Fahringer families! From High-A to AAA, it's either hotels or rent houses (that you share with as many teammates as possible to save money)."

Photo by Mark Wylie

Connor Hinchliffe

RHP ... HT: 6'2" WT: 195 ... Born: August 21, 1996, Pottsville, PA ... How Obtained: signed as an Amateur Free Agent 6/12/19 ... Attended La Salle University

Connor played the 2019 season in the Gulf Coast League.

Memory of signing

"I was notified by the local Philadelphia Area scout who called me on the phone and offered me a contract. What I remember most was how much of a roller coaster experience it was. There were times I definitely thought I'd get a shot and others when I didn't think it was possible. In the end, it worked out and I'm extremely grateful for that."

Pro debut

"I was assigned to the GCL Phillies West under Milver Reyes. I had an unforgettable first season as we won our GCL division and were paced to make a run at the championship but a hurricane canceled the end of the season. It was a very professional yet fun environment to perform in."

Life as a pro

"The difference between being a pro and an amateur is how deep the talent across an entire lineup. In college, you can lose focus a bit and still get results. In professional baseball, if you lose focus for a pitch it can get sent over the fence."

Photo by Michael Dill

Damon Jones

LHP ... HT: 6-5; WT: 240 ... Born: September 30, 1994, Twin Falls, ID ... How Obtained: 17th-round selection by Phillies in 2017 draft ... Attended Washington State University.

Damon has played at Williamsport, Lakewood, Clearwater, Reading, and Lehigh Valley. In 2020 he attended his first big league spring training and also participated in summer camp and was assigned to the Alternate Training Camp site for the season.

Memory of signing

"I was at my apartment in Pullman, WA watching the draft tracker with my then-girlfriend, now fiancé Rachel. I remember getting a call that morning that said expect to be called at some point today. I got a call in the 17th round and was asked if I'd take a certain number. I declined. I got a call again in the 18th round with a number much closer and then I became a Philadelphia Phillie."

Pro debut
"I was first assigned to the Williamsport Crosscutters. My manager was Pat Borders. I thought he was a great first manager to have. He had plenty of experience in baseball and really had his players' backs. I was extremely nervous the first time I took the mound as a professional. I want to say it took me 5 or 6 pitches to throw a strike. I'm glad I'm past that now."

Life as a pro
"I'd say the development side is one of the main differences. Being a pro, you don't have to worry about classes and homework, your sole focus is on baseball. With that being said, having less distractions helped me become fully immersed in baseball."

Life in the minors
"Being in multiple different levels now, I've seen a lot of the country I never thought I would. I'd say the more favorite ballparks I have were ones I pitched well in. I had two wonderful host families in both Williamsport and Lakewood which made those seasons that much better."

Photo by Michael Dill

Addison Russ

RHP … HT: 6'1" WT: 200 … Born: October 29, 1994, Amarillo, TX … How Obtained: 19th-round selection by Phillies in 2017 draft… Attended Houston Baptist University

Addison has played at Williamsport, Lakewood, Clearwater, and Reading. In 2020 he attended his first big league spring training and also participated in summer camp and was assigned to the Alternate Training Camp site. On August 21st he was traded to the New York Yankees for RHP David Hale.

Memory of signing

"After I saw my name pop up on the draft tracker, I was called by my area scout, Will Brunson, may he Rest in Peace. The process was fun but also made me anxious because there was so much unknown in who was going to draft me, what round, etc. Other than that, it was a once in a lifetime experience. I loved it!"

Pro debut

"After minicamp in Clearwater, I went to Williamsport for six days before going to Lakewood. My first manager was Pat Borders at Williamsport and then Marty Malloy at Lakewood so it was pretty awesome to have those guys as your manager. It was exciting. In my first game, it really didn't hit me until I looked up and realized the fans/setting of the situation. I'll never forget it!"

Life as a pro

"Being a pro is fun. I get to live my dream and play baseball every day for a living. The biggest adjustment would be ,obviously, level of play, but also the opportunities, there are so many great baseball players around you all the time so it really helps your own game just to learn from the minds around you."

Life in the minors

"I love traveling so this is an awesome chance for me to travel the country and see new places while also playing baseball. The hotels we stay in are always pretty nice. I mean there will be the bump in the road one occasionally but it's only for a few nights."

Photo by Mark Wylie

Kendall Simmons

IF … HT: 6'2" WT: 180 … Born: April 11, 2000, Macon, GA …
How Obtained: 6th-round selection by Phillies in 2018 draft
… Attended Tattnall Square Academy

Kendall has played in the Gulf Coast League and at
Williamsport.

Memory of signing

"The process was a bit stressful, as a high school senior
knowing there was a possibility of being drafted made it a big
decision as it would determine the course of my life. On
draft day I went to an old recreation ball field I used to play
at just to think about it. Afterward, I went back home to
watch the draft but fell asleep … my agent called me to tell
me I got drafted, it was a relief and the decision was made
easier by the Phillies with their offer."

Pro debut

"I played for Roly de Armas to start, he taught me so much. He's a great first coach to begin with. The first time I took the field it felt almost like travel ball until we played the Braves in Orlando and I saw their jerseys, growing up in the Atlanta area I saw the Braves a lot ... seeing their jerseys it dawned on me I was now part of being a pro player. That first year was a growing experience for me. I struggled in the beginning, and reflecting back it was good for me. I learned a lot about the game and how to approach it."

Life as a pro

"For me, pro ball simplifies things because of the attention to detail the coaches provide. As an amateur, my focus was on "big things" like home runs but in the pros, the fundamentals are stressed and it makes the game simpler to play honestly. I've learned so much in such a short time that I never knew before."

Life in the minors

"In my time at Williamsport, I shared an Extended Stay hotel room with Logan O'Hoppe. I slept on a cot ... some days were hard to stay motivated but it's a mindset to adjust and once you realize that it's not so bad. The late-night bus rides aren't fun but you adjust as well, it's all part of the process."

Photo by Cheryl Pursell

Josh Stephen

OF ... HT: 6'0" WT: 185 ... Born: September 22, 1997, Santa
Ana, CA ... How Obtained: 11th-round selection by Phillies in
2016 draft... Attended Mater Dei High School

Josh has played in the Gulf Coast League, Williamsport,
Lakewood, and Reading.

Memory of signing

"On Day Two of the draft, my agent had called and told me
the Phillies had reached out and wanted to know if I would
sign in the 11th round. The situation was right and without a
doubt, I said yes."

Pro debut

"My professional career started in Clearwater, Florida playing
for the gulf coast league Phillies. The draft had concluded
and a week later I was headed to Florida to play my first
summer of professional baseball. My first manager was Roly
de Armus and he made my first experience an experience to
remember. Taking the field as a pro for the first time is

definitely a surreal experience. One I'll never forget. I was one step closer to my dream of playing in the big leagues."

Life as a pro
"The thing that stands out to me the most about being a pro is the game of baseball is my job and life. There's no room for taking reps or days off at this level."

Life in the minors
"Throughout my career, I've stayed at some pretty cool places. The minor leagues bring you to many cities all across the country. Charleston, South Carolina is definitely my favorite city/ballpark I've been to."

Photo by Mark Wylie

DJ Stewart
IF/OF ... HT: 6'2" WT: 205 ... Born: February 2, 1999, St. Louis, MO ... How Obtained: 39th round selection by Phillies in 2017 draft ... Attended Westminster Christian Academy

DJ has played in the Gulf Coast League and at Williamsport.

Memory of signing

"The local scout called to tell me congratulations, I had been drafted by the Phillies. I then went to go look at the draft tracker and there it was, my name right next to the red Philly "P". The process was long, numerous scouts emailing and coming to watch my games. Fun, but also a bit nerve-racking. The day of the draft, my friends and I were just hanging out before practice and they were with me in the car when I got the call. It was pretty cool having friends there that I have been playing baseball with since I was six all see my dream come true."

Pro debut

"I was assigned to Rookie Ball in Clearwater, Florida for my first year playing for Roly de Armas. I was extremely nervous; I still remember how much my legs were shaking in my first pro AB. For the life of me, I could not get them to stop, but it was a surreal moment, something I will remember for the rest of my life."

Life as a pro

"The level of competition and the speed of the game is much different from high school baseball. The consistency of quality pitchers and players we face day in and day out is impressive. Everyone you play against was signed to a pro team just like me so everyone has the skill to play the game at this level.   The pace of the game is much different than high school. Even short-season A ball was faster than rookie ball. The game is just more fluid and can catch some rookies off guard."

Life in the minors

'Clearwater is a nice relaxed town, plenty of stuff to do after games or on off days. We stayed in a hotel in Clearwater so it was nice having all my teammates a thirty-second walk down the hall. It reminded me of travel baseball and being in hotels with my team. For Short-Season A ball, I was in Williamsport, PA. Unlike Clearwater, not much to do. A very small quiet town with not much going on but our team playing and the Little League World Series. My host family was really nice and took great care of me."

Photo by Michael Dill

Josh Tols

LHP ... HT: 5'7" WT: 185 ... Born: October 6, 1989, Adelaide, Australia ... How Obtained: signed as free agent 2/9/2018 ... Attended Rockhurst University

Josh has played at Clearwater, Reading, and Lehigh Valley.

Memory of signing

"I remember Howie Norsetter calling me, and either he or I had really bad service, and I could not really understand him. So, a lot of the details were missed, but he told me the Phillies were interested in signing me. I hung up the phone extremely excited but also a bit confused. He sent over my contract about two weeks later and we made it official.
It was all so surreal for me. I was 28 and had never signed with an affiliate. I thought my window had come and gone. Howie was the first scout I'd ever spoken to. It has all been a massive dream come true."

Pro debut

"I signed late February and with the international visa process taking a while, I arrived a few days late to my first spring training. I started my Phillies career in extended spring training. My first impressions were just how amazing everything was in Clearwater, the staff, the fields, the facilities. I'd waited most of my career to experience pro ball and I was not let down! My first manager was Shawn Williams in Clearwater and he's by far one of my favorite people I've met in baseball. He's a guy you'd go to war for and I've been lucky enough to play under him again throughout my career.

I remember seeing my name on the back of a Phillies uniform for the first time and I couldn't wipe the smile off my face. I take a lot of pride wearing that P on my chest. The Phillies gave me an opportunity I never thought I'd receive and I'm just trying to make the most of it. I'll never forget my first game in high A. I wouldn't say I was nervous because I felt like I had nothing to lose! Years of hard work and sacrifice all came together and I was able to prove that I belong in affiliate baseball."

Life as a pro
"The biggest difference I noticed is the size of it all. The Phillies family is a big one. There are so many different people around to help you become a big leaguer. We have so many resources at our fingertips that I couldn't even imagine when I was in college - coaches, technology, equipment, nutrition, mental skills. We have the best of it all."

Life in the minors
"Whenever I'm on the road I love finding a good coffee and some good food. I'll remember cities more if they have good coffee than if they have a nice away locker room. But I love seeing new stadiums for the first time. I'll never get sick of the view from the bullpen so it's been great to see so many stadiums and cities."

Photo by Mark Wylie

Riley Wilson

LHP … HT: 6'0" WT: 180 … Born: August 2, 1996, Midlothian, VA … How Obtained: signed as an amateur free agent 6/12/19 … Attended University of Virginia

Riley has played in the GCL.

Memory of signing

"I was at my brother's house in Charlottesville just hanging out a few days after the draft when I received a call from Kellan McKeon, who is an area scout, that the Phillies were interested in giving me a shot. I remember being extremely bummed in the time leading up to receiving that call because the draft had passed without me being selected. In the days that passed before getting that call, I was having doubts that I would get an opportunity to continue playing, but it was undoubtedly a special moment to hear those words that someone wanted to see what I could do at the next level."

Pro debut

"It was certainly different taking the mound as a pro for the first time. First and foremost, I hadn't taken the mound with anything other than "Virginia" across my chest in a long time. I also hadn't played in a "back-field" type of environment since probably high school. My last collegiate appearance was in the ACC tournament against the University of Miami, which was a high energy, high-intensity game that had a hand in determining whose season would continue into the NCAA Tournament. Compare that to the atmosphere of a GCL game, it's just a hair different, to put it mildly. So, it was certainly strange taking the mound in a game played on a backfield like that. I remember that I got smoked in my first outing, certainly an eye-opener. There were plenty of takeaways from that game though, professional hitters, especially at that level approach at-bats much different than the college guys I was previously facing. Things smoothened out after that thankfully as I made more adjustments and got used to calling my own game, something I greatly enjoy now. My first outing as a pro is certainly a memory that I can pin as the start of the professional journey."

Life as a pro

"I was assigned to the GCL upon signing, which is where I spent the entirety of my first professional season. My first manager was Milver Reyes, who was assisted by Bruce Billings, Bobby Wernes, and Ruben Gotay. Funnily enough, I had actually played against Bobby in the College World Series in 2015. He was playing at the University of Arkansas, while I was in my first year at the University of Virginia. I didn't face Bobby or anything like that, but it was still a wild coincidence. As for Milver, I greatly appreciated how he went about his business and how he handled the group of guys we had. He wanted to win, and I will fight with every fiber of my being for a manager who is fully invested in winning while backing his players. He instilled discipline in his guys, which was a pillar of the University of Virginia program in which I had just come from, so I genuinely enjoyed playing for him and how he approached coming to the field every day."

Life in the minors
"Pro ball is certainly different. Hitters have a much simpler approach, at least in the GCL, and the game generally has a much different vibe to it. The goal is always to win a championship, no matter where you are, but in the GCL development was the main priority with winning being almost a secondary reward for that development. In college, winning was paramount, College World Series or bust was the mentality."

Photo by Michael Dill

Kyle Young

LHP ... HT: 6'10" WT: 175 ... Born: December 2, 1997, Syosset, NY ... How Obtained: 22nd round selection by Phillies in 2016 draft... Attended Saint Dominic High School

Kyle played in the GCL, at Williamsport, Lakewood, and Clearwater. He had Tommy John surgery in May of 2019. He announced his retirement from professional baseball in November of 2020.

Memory of signing
"I was notified by a phone call from the area scout saying they were going to pick me next; it was an amazing feeling."

Pro debut
"I first went down to Clearwater to start with the GCL team. It was a much different experience coming from high school but it was fun! The first time I took the field I was very

nervous until I got the first pitch out of the way and then it became just like any other game."

Life as a pro
"The amount of time we put in every day on the little details was a major change for me coming from high school where practice was maybe two hours a day."

Life in the minors
"What makes it different is the talent and work ethic needed to perform and get better every day."

Photo by Michael Dill

Mike Ventola
Media Relations Manager and broadcaster - Lehigh Valley Iron Pigs

Director of Public/Media Relations & Broadcaster (2014-2018)

Phillies Experience

"My first experience with the Philadelphia Phillies organization was being a game-day worker in the press box for the Reading Phillies during the 2010 season. Media Relations Director Tommy Viola hired me to help out around the press box filling various roles such as keeping stats and making sure the writers and press box workers were good with everything they needed. I even interviewed players for the website! It was a great first experience in the Phillies organization.

It continued into next season when I was hired to be pre-game and post-game show host for the Lehigh Valley IronPigs on the IronPigs Radio Network. The 2011 season was the most successful season for the IronPigs, making it all the way to the International League Championship Series against the Columbus Clippers (they sadly lost).

Those two stops (and others) led me back to Reading where I became their radio announcer in the 2014 season and stayed there through the end of the 2018 season. It was such a thrill for me, especially getting hired out of Independent Baseball. My time in Reading prepared me for the role I'm with now with the Lehigh Valley IronPigs - as their media relations manager and broadcaster."

Memory of first pro broadcasting job

"I got goosebumps up and down my arms and it felt like it was a dream. My first lead role as an announcer was with the Southern Illinois Miners of the Frontier League in 2012. I remember walking into Bosse Field in Evansville, Indiana for an exhibition game and it was my first game broadcasting baseball as a solo/lead announcer. Bosse Field is where they filmed the movie A League of Their Own, so it really felt like I had hit a home run. That season was so crucial for me in my development as a professional because the team won the championship that season. It allowed me to be a part of the highs and lows that go into a season. I got to see remarkable and memorable wins and devastating losses that at times looked as if the team wouldn't make the postseason."

Pro Baseball debut
"My first experience in professional baseball was during the 2009 season when I was an intern with the Augusta GreenJackets, the single-A affiliate of the San Francisco Giants. I was a promotions intern and also got the opportunity to broadcast a few games on the radio alongside their radio announcer. It was that summer that confirmed my desire to chase my dream of becoming a professional broadcaster. It allowed me to see a different part of the country I had never been to before and allowed me to get my feet wet in the day-to-day operations of professional baseball."

Life as a pro
"The relationship-building you develop with the coaches and players in uniform plus the fans. It's what I enjoy most about working in professional baseball. I've been blessed to work not only as a radio announcer but as a media relations contact as well. As a media relations contact, I have to prepare daily game notes, roster updates, stats packs, and make sure all media obligations are filled prior to the first pitch. I help set up interviews and even conduct interviews as well. I write press releases on behalf of the organization, be it in a non-baseball or baseball release. I've enjoyed that

aspect of the job because it's helped me become a better announcer.

I get a front row view every day of not only talking and working with the players but get to call the high points (and low points) of their careers. I get to ride shotgun on their journeys. I've had the privilege of meeting their significant others, family members, kids, and even friends of theirs when they come to the ballpark. I also get emails and Facebook messages as well from time to time. I cherish those greatly. Also, when it comes to the fans - without fans, I don't have a job! They are what keep me going!"

Life in the minors
"I love traveling with the team because you get a chance to see so many great ballparks outside of your own park. The Phillies affiliates have great stadiums, be it Coca-Cola Park, FirstEnergy Stadium, Spectrum Field, and FirstEnergy Park. All of these parks have great layouts plus outstanding atmospheres. When traveling, you get a chance to see what the rest of baseball looks like!"

Photo courtesy of Kirsten Karbach

Kirsten Karbach
Manager of Communications & Impact - Pitch for Baseball & Softball

Director of Public/Media Relations & Broadcaster - Reading Fightins (2019), Clearwater Threshers broadcaster (2014-2018). 2018 Florida State League broadcaster of the year.

Phillies Experience
"I began an unpaid internship with the Clearwater Threshers in May of 2013, just after graduating from the University of South Florida. This was the first year that Clearwater had employed a broadcaster to provide play-by-play (Ben Gellman-Chomsky), and Ben brought me on to join him as the team's second broadcaster. I handled color commentary and middle-innings play-by-play for home games and local road games that year, and even got to do a few solo broadcasts for road games in Fort Myers and Brevard County. With Ben not returning the following year, I was offered the

opportunity to be the team's play-by-play broadcaster, and I held that position for five seasons."

Memory of first pro broadcasting job
"I actually don't have much recollection of the first professional game I worked, or my first game as a paid professional. But I do remember 2014 being an exciting year, as it was my first season as a lead play-by-play broadcaster in professional baseball. The Threshers didn't win their 10th game until late May and only won 17 games in the first half, but I had an absolute blast that season."

Pro Baseball debut
"My professional career as a broadcaster technically began when I was hired by the Threshers in 2014, but I did have a few seasons of experience in Minor League Baseball prior to that. In 2011 I wrote a couple of game recaps and did color commentary for a few games with the Dunedin Blue Jays. In 2012 I interned with the Charlotte Stone Crabs in broadcasting and media relations under Grant McAuley, who now hosts pre- and post-game shows for the Atlanta Braves Radio Network. Grant always ran a very professional and informative broadcast, and almost everything I knew about producing a quality broadcast I learned from him. I split my time between working a part-time job in Tampa and interning from 10 a.m. to 11 p.m. or so for home games in Port Charlotte that summer, so it was here where I really began to learn about the dedication it takes to work in MiLB."

Life as a pro
"It's fascinating, challenging, exhausting, and exhilarating. Outside of the industry, most people

assume that broadcasters show up a couple of hours before game time, call the game, and leave right after the post-game show. But broadcasting in Minor League Baseball is much more demanding. Usually, the broadcaster will also handle Game Notes (which can take several hours), compiling and distributing stat packs and rosters to coaches and media, website editing, social media, fulfilling media requests, scheduling and conducting interviews, game recaps, and writing press releases, to name a few. In Clearwater, I also recorded radio spots and produced the broadcast (as it was online-only and not through a radio station), wrote copy, and did the on-camera work for promotional ads and other in-stadium videos. I loved all of the work I did. But it was a lot. For home games, a 12-hour day is pretty typical, and a full day off during the summer is rare."

Life in the minors
"In the Florida State League, a lot of our opponents were a short commute away, so we would not have to stay overnight. I either rode the bus with the team or drove my own car to these games. For the most part, the Threshers would only broadcast home and local road games, but I did do a few overnight trips for playoff games and a couple key series later in my career there. The hotels were usually Holiday Inns or something similar. Daytona's was definitely my favorite; it was a Holiday Inn on the beach. As far as the stadiums, you can't beat Spectrum Field in Clearwater. In my one year in Reading, I went on road trips to Harrisburg, Portland, New Hampshire, Bowie, Akron, Binghamton, Hartford, and Trenton. I honestly most enjoyed those with food within walking distance or a good hotel breakfast. Dunkin Donuts Park in Hartford is a top-notch stadium, and I

loved that Hadlock Field in Portland always had coffee in the press box."

Photo by Michael Dill

Greg Giombarrese
Director of Communications & Radio Broadcaster - Lakewood Blue Claws

Phillies Experience
"I joined the BlueClaws in 2007 as an intern in the media/broadcast department under Ben Wagner, now the radio voice of the Blue Jays. I started in January, but Ben left in March to go work for the Buffalo Bisons. Brendan Burke, now the TV voice of the New York Islanders, joined up and we worked together for that year. I was not here in 2008, but came back for the 2009 season and have been here ever since.

My first BlueClaws game was actually one of the most memorable. The year prior, 2006, the BlueClaws had won their first South Atlantic League Championship. So, Opening

Night of 2007 featured the raising of the championship banner. It also featured...winter. It was about 38 degrees and very windy, with snow flurries, as the game got underway. The BlueClaws starting pitcher that night was a right-hander named Carlos Monasterios, who had never pitched, nor probably set foot in, temperatures anywhere near as cold as it was that night. Considering the weather, the crowd at the start of the game was great. They cheered loudly as the banner was raised...and then most of them went home after Greensboro scored nine runs in the top of the first inning."

Memory of first pro broadcasting job
"My first job in baseball was with the River City Rascals in 2004, based in the St. Louis suburb of O'Fallon, Missouri working in the independent Frontier League. Their broadcaster, Phil Giubileo, was a Fordham grad and brought me out to serve as his number two broadcaster. I was in college at the time and was out there from around Memorial Day through mid-August when I came back east to start the fall semester.

It was a lot of fun, but a bit different and more laid back than working for the BlueClaws would be a few years later. As an intern, I did not have that much responsibility, but definitely learned a lot and gained valuable experience on the air, doing interviews, working with players and coaches, and being a part of a daily broadcast."

Pro Baseball debut
"Being on the air was great of course, but by that time I had a lot of on-air experience from college and elsewhere. I was actually a bit more nervous for the additional job requirements leading into the season but once we got rolling

all was well. There's nothing quite like being on the air, calling a big home run or late-inning drama with a packed house and the game on the line. It's quite exhilarating."

Life as a pro
"Every year is a bit different but one of the highlights of each season is the interaction with the players and the coaches. Most everyone that I've gotten to work with over the years has been great. In the case of the coaches and the coordinators, I love just picking up conversations with them one year that we had the year before.

In my role, I am involved in any external communication and messaging that comes from the BlueClaws, including but not limited to social media, advertising, our website, media relations, email marketing, select graphic design, and database management.

While all that keeps me busy, certainly my favorite part of the job is sitting down behind the microphone at 7:05 each night."

Life in the minors
"We stay with the team in their hotel. Each ballpark is a little different, but that's one of the best parts about baseball. In the Sally League, my favorite stadium is Greenville in South Carolina. They are a Red Sox affiliate, so their Mini Monster is a natural fit, but additionally, they don't overwhelm you with advertisements all over the place and the park has a natural, old-time charm to it.

Asheville, in North Carolina, is also beautiful. It's the oldest park in the league, but was heavily renovated a few years ago. McCormick Field is built into the side of a mountain, so it's very small (pitchers hate it), but again, like Greenville, it has an amazing old-time charm. In an era of modern ballparks, this 90 plus-year-old stadium is as good a place to watch a game as any in Minor League Baseball."

Photo by Barb Potter

Gary Kay

We would be remiss if we didn't include some thoughts on the "lost season" of 2020. Every professional baseball-related job was altered in some shape or form due to COVID concerns ... many were even furloughed till further notice. One of the areas that remained a consistent need regardless of the reduction of baseball activities was security at the ballparks and complexes.

At the Carpenter Complex in Clearwater, there is a small shed located alongside the entranceway. It's one of the primary areas where the security team maintains a close watch over the training facility. When the Complex entry gates closed to visitors as baseball shut down due to the pandemic, the security team took on additional duties to ensure the safety of folks working within the fences.

Gary Kay is the Security Team Lead at Carpenter Complex; he's been a Phillies employee since 2014. As the summer played out here was his perspective in regards to the safeguarding that took place and also a cool fact ... he's very involved with Little League Baseball.

The Job

"Ensuring that players, staff, and guests have a safe environment when they are at the Complex. Initially, we do this by monitoring all entry to the Complex using metal detectors and bag checks for everyone that comes thru the pedestrian gate. We also monitor gates and building entrances within the Complex to ensure they are closed to unauthorized personnel."

Interaction

"We interact with players, coaches, and staff on a daily basis when they enter or exit the premises to start/end their day. I also see them around the offices, clubhouse, and the fields when I'm monitoring inside the complex. Prior to my role at Carpenter Complex, I was one of the security team members that worked the Player/Staff parking lot at Spectrum Field where I interacted with the Major League team and staff."

Added duties during the Pandemic

"Logging in and out the players and staff when they reported each day. We also take and record their temperatures upon arrival. We have a collection box at the security shed on the days that they take a COVID test. All who entered the complex and were there for an extended period were required to put their test sample in the box before entering."

Baseball and Little League

"I've been a baseball fan since I was a little kid, sure wish my old baseball cards didn't get thrown away! I really got into the game in 1979 when I got involved coaching a Little League Team in Ft Wayne, IN. I enjoy the strategy of the game.

I got involved in Little League in 1979 when a neighbor boy told me he was on a Little League team but, unless they found someone to coach the team they couldn't play. I volunteered to help and have been involved ever since, I've coached, umpired, served as a League Official, have overseen tournaments, etc.

I was transferred from Ft. Wayne, IN to Largo, FL for my job in 2003. I continued to volunteer in my local district here; the Little League Southern Regional was held in Gulfport, FL at the time. I visited the Little League World Series (which was on my bucket list) in 1993, it was such an exciting event I wanted to be a part of it … in 1994 I started volunteering as an usher and have been volunteering in Williamsport, PA every year since.

The Little League Classic has been a big hit for both the major leaguers and the little leaguers. The major leaguers get to spend time during the day at the World Series interacting with the kids and that evening the kids get to go to the big-

119

league game as their guest. I think the major leaguers enjoy it as much as the youngsters do. Smiles all around!"

Triple A Level

Triple-A is the highest minor league level, one step away from the major leagues. There have been three such leagues in the history of minor league baseball in the states. The International League was established in 1886 without classification, deemed a D league for one season (1908), then AA (1912-45), and AAA starting in 1946. The Pacific Coast League was founded in 1903 as a six-team league involving cities in California, Oregon, and Washington. The American Association operated primarily in the Midwest and South-Central U. S. from 1902-62 and 1969-97.

The earliest baseball-reference.com lists the Phillies as having a Triple-A affiliate is 1948, the Toronto Maple Leafs in the International League. They've fielded teams in each of the three leagues but exclusively in the International League since 1987.

Chronology of AAA Affiliations
Toronto, CA – 1948 to 1950 – International League
Baltimore, MD – 1951 to 1953 – International League
Syracuse, NY – 1954 to 1955 – International League
Miami, FL – 1956 to 1958 – International League
Buffalo, NY – 1959 to 1962 – International League
Indianapolis, IN – 1960 – American Association
Dallas/Ft. Worth, TX 1962 – American Association
Little Rock, AK – 1963 to 1965 – American Association
San Diego, CA – 1966 to 1968 – Pacific Coast League
Eugene, OR - 1969 to 1973 - Pacific Coast League
Toledo, OH - 1974 to 1975 - International League
Oklahoma City, OK - 1976 to 1982 - American Association
Portland, OR - 1983 to 1986 - Pacific Coast League
Old Orchard Beach, ME - 1987 to 1988 - International League

Scranton/Wilkes-Barre, PA - 1989 to 2006 - International
League
Ottawa, ON, CA - 2007 - International League
Allentown, PA - 2008 to Present - International League

Toronto Maple Leafs

The Toronto Maple Leafs pro baseball team existed from
1896 to 1967. For three years, the Maple Leafs were the
Phillies top minor league club, 1948-50.

Ballpark
Maple Leaf Stadium. Opening day was April 29, 1926. It was
demolished in 1968.

Managers
Eddie Sawyer, Dick Porter (1948), Del Bissonette (1949), Jack
Sanford (1950).

Climbing the Ladder
Players who went on to five-plus years in the majors: (1948)
RHP Bubba Church, 3B Willie Jones, RHP Jim Konstanty, C
Stan Lopata, RHP Lou Possehl, LHP Jocko Thompson, RHP
Steve Ridzik; (1949) 3B Mike Goliat, INF Putsy Caballero;
(1950) OF Jackie Mayo.

Team Notes
Manager Eddie Sawyer, who joined the Phillies organization
in 1944 as the Utica skipper, began 1948 in Toronto before
being promoted to the Phillies on July 26, 1948. Two years
later the Whiz Kids, a young group of home-grown Phillies,
won the National League pennant. All of the above players
except Possehl played for Sawyer that season with

Jones, Lopata, Konstanty, and Goliat playing major roles. Konstanty won the National League MVP Award.

Baltimore Orioles

Long before the current American League Orioles, Baltimore was home to minor league baseball. The name was always the Orioles, as far back as 1903 when Baltimore was in the Eastern League. The Phillies spent three seasons with Baltimore as their affiliate in the AAA International League (1951-53). In 1954, the St. Louis Browns relocated to Baltimore, a city that was a charter member of the American League (1901-02).

The Orioles were one of 12 Phillies minor league clubs in 1951.

Ballpark
Memorial Stadium.

Managers
Nick Cullop (1951), Don Heffner (1952-53).

Climbing the Ladder
(1951) 2B Mike Goliat, C Stan Lopata, OF Jackie Mayo, RHP Steve Ridzik; (1952) RHP Bob Miller, INF Ted Kazanski; (1953) INF Putsy Caballero, RHP Jack Sanford.

Syracuse Chiefs

The franchise was established in 1934 when the Jersey City Skeeters club moved to Syracuse. The initial team played in the International League through 1955, including two seasons as a Phillies affiliate, 1954-55.

Ballpark
MacArthur Stadium. Built in 1934, named after General
Douglass MacArthur eight years later and razed in 1997.

Manager
Skeeter Newsome.

Climbing the Ladder
(1954) OF Bob Bowman, RHP Jack Meyer, RHP Jim Owens,
RHP Jack Sanford; (1955) OF Mel Clark, RHP Turk Farrell, LHP
Seth Morehead.

Team Notes
Owens, a hard-throwing 20-year-old, was second in the IL in
wins (17-8), his first year in AAA (1954); fourth in ERA (2.87),
second in innings (223), led in walks (127), second in
strikeouts (150) and shared the high mark in shutouts (5) …
Meyer led league in strikeouts (173) the same year.

Miami Marlins
There were two stints of minor league baseball associated
with the Phillies and Miami, FL. In 1956, the AAA level
Syracuse Chiefs franchise moved to Miami and became the
Marlins. The Phillies maintained their affiliation with the AAA
version of the Marlins, 1956-58. It was truly an International
League as it included franchises in Montreal (Royals), Toronto
(Maple Leafs) and Havana (Sugar Kings).

The Phillies second Miami minor league stint came in 1962
when the Class A Florida State League resurrected the Miami
Hustlers franchise and renamed it the Marlins to honor the
defunct AAA franchise. (See Class A chapter)

In 1993 the expansion Florida Marlins joined the National League; they became the Miami Marlins in 2011.

Ballpark
Miami Stadium. The stadium was built in 1949 and was known for its cantilevered grandstand with no support beams which meant there were no unobstructed views of the field. The stadium was razed in 1999.

Managers
Don Osborne (1956-57), Kerby Ferrell (1958).

Climbing the Ladder
(1956) 1B Ed Bouchee, OF Bob Bowman, OF Mel Clark, RHP Don Cardwell, RHP Jim Owens, RHP Turk Farrell, LHP Seth Morehead; (1957) RHP Bubba Church, OF Chuck Essegian, RHP Jack Meyer, RHP Dallas Green; (1958) RHP Bob Miller.

Team Notes
Incredible ageless Satchel Paige, although not property of the Phillies, pitched all three years; 10-10 in the third season at age 51 ... INF Whitey Herzog was Phillies property in 1957. He went on to become a Hall of Fame manager ... C Haywood Sullivan was on the same club as Herzog. Sullivan wound up as GM, CEO, COO of the Red Sox.

Buffalo Bisons
The Buffalo Bisons are one of the most storied franchises in minor league baseball history. Originating in 1877 as a member of the League Alliance (the first semi-affiliated minor league) the franchise briefly became a major league team in the National League, 1879-85; back to the minors, 1886-89; charter member of the American League (1901-02);

126

back to the minors (1903-70); out of baseball (1971-78) but returned to minor league ball (1979). They've always been the Bisons.

The Phillies affiliated with Buffalo in the International League, 1959-62.

Ballparks
Offerman Stadium. Built in 1924 and demolished after the 1960 season. The Phillies played there, 1959-60. War Memorial Stadium was home to the Phillies, 1961-62.

Manager
Kerby Ferrell.

Climbing the Ladder
(1959) INF Ruben Amaro Sr., RHP Turk Farrell, RHP Dallas Green, RHP Art Mahaffey, LHP Chris Short, OF Bobby Del Greco; (1960) OF Bob Bowman, SS Bobby Wine; (1961) 1B Don Mincher, OF Ted Savage; (1962) LHP Dennis Bennett, OF Danny Cater, INF Lee Elia, OF John Herrnstein, RHP Fergie Jenkins, LHP Marcelino Lopez.

Team Notes
(1959) 1B Pancho Herrera won the league's MVP and Triple Crown (.329 average, 37 home runs, 128 RBI). Had a short, three-season career with the Phillies (1958, 1960-61) ... (1961) OF Ted Savage won the IL MVP, .325; led in OBP (.427) and stolen bases (31).

Indianapolis Indians

Twice the Phillies had two AAA teams. The first year was 1960 when they had a working agreement with the Buffalo Bisons but also a one-year PDC with the Indianapolis Indians (American Association).

Managers
Johnny Hutchings, Ted Beard.

Ballpark
Victory Field.

Climbing the Ladder
INF Ruben Amaro Sr., RHP Bobby Locke, LHP Chris Short.

Dallas/Fort Worth Rangers

The second time was 1962, Buffalo and a split working agreement with the Los Angeles Angels fo the Dallas/Ft. Worth Rangers franchise (American Association).

Fun Fact
Did you know that the original name of the NFL Dallas Cowboys was to be the Rangers? They changed it to the Cowboys to avoid confusion with the then-existing Dallas Rangers minor league baseball club.

Ballpark
LaGrave Field – Fort Worth.

Managers
Dick Littlefield, Ray Murray.

Climbing the Ladder
C Pat Corrales, 2B Cookie Rojas, RHP Dwight Siebler.

Team Notes
Two players who were the property of the Angels were on the roster, SS Jim Fregosi and OF Chuck Tanner. Both went onto outstanding careers as managers in the majors ... Phillies INF Wayne Graham had a short stint in the majors but wound up as a very successful baseball coach at Rice University.

Arkansas Travelers
With the official restructuring of minor league baseball in 1963, the Phillies started a three-year affiliation with the Arkansas Travelers in Little Rock, AK, a city that had been without baseball the previous two years. The Travelers were in the International League (1963) and the Pacific Coast League the other two years of the working agreement with the Phillies.

Travelers is the second-longest-running nickname in minor league baseball history behind the Buffalo Bisons. Ironically, the Phillies had been in Buffalo for four seasons before moving to Little Rock.

Ballpark
Traveler Field. Renamed Ray Winder Field (1966). Final season, 2006. Field was sold to the University of Arkansas, razed in 2012 for a parking lot. The scoreboard was saved and remains as it was for all those years.

Manager
Frank Lucchesi.

Climbing the Ladder
(1963), OF Dick Allen, INF-OF Danny Cater, INF Lee Elia, OF John Herrnstein, RHP Ferguson Jenkins, RHP Jack Hamilton, LHP Marcelino Lopez, RHP Dwight Siebler; (1964) C Pat Corrales, RHP Dallas Green, OF Alex Johnson, LHP John Morris, OF Adolfo Phillips, RHP Gary Wagner; (1965) LHP Grant Jackson, RHP Rick Wise.

Team Notes
Allen, 21, had a monster season, his last in the minors. He led the league in triples (12), home runs (33), RBI (97), total bases (299) while hitting .289. Surprisingly Dick shared the team-high with three sacrifice bunts. Allen's four-year minor league career: 88 doubles, 40 triples, 81 homers, 342 RBI, .305 average . . . Lee Elia played two seasons as did Dallas Green. Both wound up managing the Phillies . . . Jenkins was enshrined into the National Baseball Hall of Fame and Museum (1991).

San Diego Padres
The San Diego Padres have been in the National League since 1969. Prior to that, the Padres were the Phillies AAA affiliate in the Pacific Coast League for three seasons, 1966-68.

The road to minor league baseball in San Diego took a lot of turns. It began with the 1903 Sacramento club, which over time, moved to Tacoma, back to Sacramento, San Francisco, Salt Lake City, Los Angeles as the Hollywood Stars, and finally to San Diego in 1936. The Red Sox had a working agreement with San Diego that year. A 17-year-old outfielder made his pro debut, hitting .271 in 42 games, Ted Williams.

Ballparks
The Phillies club played in Westgate Park the first two seasons and the newly built San Diego Stadium in 1968, the city's final minor league season.

Managers
Fran Lucchesi (1966), Bob Skinner (1967-68,) and Bobby Klaus (1968). Skinner left during the 1968 season to replace Gene Mauch as the Phillies manager. Lucchesi later managed the Phillies.

Climbing the Ladder
SS Larry Bowa, OF Larry Hisle, LHP Grant Jackson, 3B Rick Joseph, RHP Barry Lersch, SS Don Money, 2B Gary Sutherland, RHPs Gary Wagner, Bill Wilson, Rick Wise ... Among the veterans, LHP Bo Belinski, RHP Dallas Green, 1B Jim Gentile, C Doc Edwards, C Jimmie Schaffer, RHP Ed Roebuck.

Team Notes
The 1967 team (85-63) defeated the Spokane Indians in the Championship Series.

Eugene Emeralds
When the San Diego Padres became an expansion team in the National League (1969), the Phillies moved their AAA Pacific Coast League affiliate from San Diego up to Eugene, OR. The Phillies were there 1969-73. Twice before the Phillies had affiliations in Eugene. See Class A and Short-Season chapters later in this book.

131

Ballpark
Civic Stadium. In 1969 concurrent with Eugene's move to AAA, Civic Stadium became the new home for the Phillies. The stadium had been solely used for football the previous 20 years. Significant updates were made prior to the Emeralds taking the field. The ballpark had been originally built in 1938.

Managers
Frank Lucchesi (1969), Bob Wellman-Lou Kahn (1970), Andy Seminick (1971-72), Jim Bunning (1973).

Won division but lost Championship Series to Tacoma Cubs, 3-1 (1969). Lost playoffs to Albuquerque Dukes, 3-1 (1971).

Climbing the Ladder
(1969) SS Larry Bowa, RHP Billy Champion, 2B Denny Doyle, RHP Barry Lersch, RHP Gary Wagner. (1970) OF Oscar Gamble, RHP Mike Jackson, OF Joe Lis, 1B William Montanez, LHP Ken Reynolds, 3B John Vukovich. (1971) OF Mike Anderson, OF Larry Hisle, 1B Greg Luzinski, RHP Wayne Twitchell. (1972) C Bob Boone, OF Bill Robinson, OF Mike Rogodzinski, 2B Mike Schmidt, LHP Mac Scarce. (1973) RHP Larry Christenson.

Team Notes
Playing under Andy Seminick, Boone spent his first full minor league season as a catcher. Schmidt played most of his AAA year at second base. Batting champion with a .372 average in 1971 Portland outfielder Charlie Manuel.

Over the 10 total years in Eugene: two future Hall of Famers wore an Emeralds uniform (Bunning, Schmidt), a 1974 Cy Young Award winner (Mike Marshall), a broadcaster with the Blue Jays (Martinez), two managers (Bowa, Boone) and six members of the 1980 World Champion Phillies (Bowa, Vukovich, Luzinski, Boone, Schmidt, Christenson).

Toledo Mud Hens

Toledo, OH, has a long history of minor league baseball and teams in a host of different level leagues. The Phillies called Toledo home of their triple-A teams in the International League for two years, 1974-75. The team originally played in Bay View Park, which was located near marshland inhabited by wildlife birds known as "American Coots"; also known as "mud hens." For this reason, the local press soon dubbed the team the "Mud Hens".

Ballpark

Ned Skeldon Stadium. Originally named Lucas County Stadium, opened in 1965. Previously it was a horse racetrack dating back to 1902.

Manager

Jim Bunning.

Climbing the Ladder

RHP Larry Christenson, RHP Gene Garber, C Jim Essian, OF Jay Johnstone, OF Jerry Martin, OF Mike Rogodzinski, LHP Willie Hernandez, RHP Dick Ruthven, and 3B John Vukovich.

Oklahoma City 89ers

For a seven-year period (1976-82), the Phillies AAA affiliate was the Oklahoma City (OK) 89ers club. Since the reclassification of the minor leagues in 1963, it was the only time the Phillies fielded a team in the American Association. The franchise's original name referred to the land run of 1889 which led to the founding of Oklahoma City.

Ballpark

All-Sports Stadium was built in 1958 and was primarily used for baseball. It was also a popular outdoor concert venue. The stadium was closed in 1997 and demolished in 2005.

Managers

Jim Bunning (1976), Cal Emery, Mike Ryan, Billy Connors (1977), Mike Ryan (1978), Lee Elia (1979), Jim Snyder (1980-81), Ron Clark, Tony Taylor, Cot Deal (1982).

Climbing the Ladder

(1976) RHP Dan Boitano, OF Rick Bosetti, LHP Willie Hernandez, 1B Dane Iorg, LHP Randy Lerch, 3B Jim Morrison, C Bill Nahorodny, OF Lonnie Smith. (1977) RHP Warren Brusstar, RHP Billy Champion, C Keith Moreland, RHP Jim Wright. (1978) OF Mike Anderson, INF Ramon Aviles, LHP Kevin Saucier, 3B John Vukovich. (1979) RHP Marty Bystrom, 1B Len Matuszek, RHP Dickie Noles. (1980) INF Luis Aguayo, RHP Bob Walk. (1981) OF Bob Dernier, INF Ryne Sandberg, C Ozzie Virgil, OF George Vukovich, LHP Mark Davis. (1982) SS Julio Franco, 1B Willie Montanez, RHP Jerry Reed, OF Alejandro Sanchez, LHP Don Carman.

Team Notes

(1978) Smith led the AA in stolen bases (66) ... (1981) Dernier led the AA in stolen bases (72) ... Smith, Moreland, Bystrom, Noles and Walk all made significant contributions to the 1980 WS Champion Phillies.

Portland Beavers

For four seasons, 1983-86, the Phillies AAA affiliate was in Portland, OR, in the Northern Division of a 10-team Pacific Coast League.

In 1919 an expansion franchise in Portland was created entitled the Beavers ... Actor Bing Russell created the Portland Mavericks for the 1973 season, an independent team in the short-season Northwest League. Russell later sold his territorial rights for a record $206,000 in 1978 when MLB brought the PCL back to Portland ... A documentary entitled "The Battered Bastards of Baseball" debuted in 2014 detailing the club's brief existence - 5 years - 4 Division titles.

Ballpark

Civic Stadium was the ballpark in which the Beavers played. Name was later changed to PGE Park. Originally built in 1926. Used exclusively for football until 1956 when it became home to Portland's various pro baseball franchises.

Managers

John Felske (1983), Lee Elia (1984), Bill Dancy (1985-86). All three wound up coaching in the majors with the Phillies. Felske and Elia also managed the Phils.

(1983) Portland defeated the Edmonton Trappers in the playoffs, 3-1, and swept the Albuquerque Dukes in the Championship Series, 3-0.

Climbing the Ladder
(1983) INF Luis Aguayo, INF Ramon Aviles, RHP Kevin Gross, RHP Charles Hudson, SS Steve Jeltz, 1B Len Matuszek, C John Russell, 2B Juan Samuel, 3B Rick Schu. (1984) RHP Marty Bystrom, LHP Don Carman, C Darren Daulton, OF Jeff Stone. (1985) OF Chris James, LHP Randy Lerch. (1986) Ron Jones, Joe Lefebvre, Milt Thompson.

Team Notes
Larry Andersen, a 30-year-old reliever pitched there in 1983, his third time in a Beavers uniform (1978, 1980). The Phillies purchased his contract on July 26, 1983.

Maine Guides
After being in Portland, OR, for four years, the Phillies moved their AAA affiliate to the east coast in Old Orchard Beach, ME in the International League for 1987-88. The ball club was named the Guides from 1984-87 in honor of Maine's hunting and wilderness guides. Name was changed to the Maine Phillies in 1988.

Ballpark
The Ballpark. In 1983 new Maine Guides owner Jordan Kobritz oversaw the construction of a new Old Orchard Beach baseball stadium, called the Ball Park on the outskirts of town.

Managers
Bill Dancy (1987) and George Culver (1988).

Climbing the Ladder
(1987) C Darren Daulton, RHP Marvin Freeman, RHP Todd Frohwirth, OF Chris James, NF Steve Jeltz, RHP Michael Jackson, OF Ron Jones, RHP Mike Maddux, OF Ron Roenicke, C John Russell, OF Jeff Stone. (1988) RHP Marty Bystrom, 1B Ricky Jordan, LHP Wally Ritchie, RHP Scott Service.

Scranton/Wilkes-Barre Red Barons
Since the 1963 reorganization, the Phillies triple-A franchise was in several locations all west of the Mississippi River, except 1987-88 when the Maine Guides joined the International League. In 1989, the team's top farm team moved to northeastern Pennsylvania, the Scranton/Wilkes-Barre Red Barons. It remained there through 2006.

Ballpark
Lackawanna County Stadium located in Moosic, PA. Opened in 1989 as the new home of the Red Barons. It was designed as a mini version of Veterans Stadium in Philadelphia with an artificial turf surface.

Managers
Bill Dancy (1989-91), Lee Elia (1992), George Culver (1993), Mike Quade (1994-95), Ramon Aviles (1996), Butch Hobson (1996), Marc Bombard (1997-2001p 2002-04), Jerry Martin (2001), Gene Lamont (2005), John Russell (2006).

(1992) Won Eastern Division (84-58), lost Championship Series to Columbus . . . (2000) Won Eastern Division (85-60); lost Championship to Indianapolis . . . (2001) Won Eastern Division (78-65); lost championship to Louisville, 1-0; series cancelled after one game . . . (2002) Third straight division

title (91-53); lost to Buffalo . . . (2006) Another division title
(84-58); lost to Rochester in finals.

Climbing the Ladder

Pitchers
Bruce Ruffin, Todd Frohwirth, Marvin Freeman, Chuck
McElroy, Jeff Tabaka, Bob Sebra, Jason Grimsley, Jay Baller,
Mike Williams, Toby Borland, Bob Wells, Larry Andersen, Paul
Quantrill, Mike Grace, Bobby Munoz, Wayne Gomes, Randy
Wolf, Adam Eaton, Dickie Noles, Tommy Greene, Mike
Maddux, Andy Ashby, Ricky Bottalico, Tyler Green, Brandon
Duckworth, Gavin Floyd, Geoff Geary, Brett Myers, Ryan
Madson, Cole Hamels, J.A. Happ, Vicente Padilla, Amaury
Telemaco, Vicente Padilla, Clay Condrey.

Catchers
Darren Daulton, Darrin Fletcher, Todd Pratt, Mike Lieberthal,
Gary Bennett, Bobby Estalella, Chris Coste, Carlos Ruiz,
Johnny Estrada.

Infielders
Charlie Hayes, Kim Batiste, Von Hayes, Dave Hollins,
Steve Scarsone, Mickey Morandini, Ricky Jordan, Kevin
Stocker, Rick Schu, Kevin Jordan, Scott Rolen, Kevin Sefcik,
Jimmy Rollins, Marlon Anderson, Nick Punto, Chase Utley,
Ryan Howard. (Utley's first season—2002—found him
playing 3B; next year he was back at 2B).

Outfielders

138

Wes Chamberlain, Ruben Amaro Jr., Jeff Stone, Tony Longmire, Pat Burrell, Jason Michaels, Marlon Byrd, Shane Victorino, Michael Bourn, Eric Valent.

Ottawa Lynx

The Phillies AAA team in 2007 was in Ottawa, Ontario, a city that had been in the International League since 1993. Following the 2006 season, owner Ray Pecor sold the franchise to Joe Finley and Craig Stein, while Pecor maintained a minority stake. The plan was to relocate the franchise to Allentown, PA, but a stadium needed to be built.

The Ottawa Lynx played their final season in 2007, finishing with the league's worst record (55-88). The following year, the Lehigh Valley Iron Pigs became the Phillies' top farm team.

Ballpark
Raymond Chabot Grant Thornton Park. The stadium opened prior to the 1993 Lynx season.

Manager
John Russell.

Climbing the Ladder
C Chris Coste, LHP J.A. Happ, and RHP Clay Condrey were all on the World Champion Phillies the following year. C Dusty Wathan ended his playing career and began a managerial career the next season in Williamsport.

Lackawanna County Stadium - photo by Dave Schofield

Moosic, PA, SWB fans: Dave Schofield

Moosic, PA, Lackawanna County Stadium: Dave Schofield

Eugene, OR, Civic Stadium: ballparkreviews.com

Oklahoma City, OK, All-Sports Stadium: Charles O'Reilly

Old Orchard Beach, ME, The Ballpark: Charles O'Reilly

Little Rock, AR, Ray Winder Field: Charles O'Reilly

Syracuse, NY, MacArthur Stadium: Charles O'Reilly

Ottawa Lynx, sportslogos.net

Maine Guides, sportslogos.net

Scranton/Wilkes-Barre Red Barons, sportslogos.net

Lehigh Valley Iron Pigs

The Lehigh Valley IronPigs' origins date back to 1993 and the Ottawa Lynx. In 2008, the franchise moved to Allentown. The IronPigs have been extremely well received given the Phillies' large fan base.

Ballpark

Coca-Cola Park. Groundbreaking ceremonies for the new ballpark were held in September of 2006 and construction was completed in February 2008. The layout is slightly different from most ballparks, as the main entrance is located on the right field line rather than the common location behind home plate. Fans with club seating tickets, however, do have a designated entrance behind home plate. The field's dimensions closely match those of the Phillies' home field Citizens Bank Park with a distance of 334 feet to left, 400 feet to center, and 325 to right.

Managers
Dave Huppert (2008-10), Ryne Sandberg (2011-12), Dave Brundage (2013-16), Dusty Wathan (2017), Gary Jones (2018-19).

Climbing the Ladder
(2008) Andy Tracy led the club with 22 home runs and 85 RBI... Mike Cervenak (.311) and Brandon Watson (.305) hit over .300 as regulars ... RJ Swindle posted a 1.98 ERA, 27 G, 36 IP.

(2009) Mike Cervenak hit .305, 119 games ... Andy Tracy hit 26 homers with 96 RBI ... Kyle Kendrick went 9-7 with a 3.34 ERA, 24 starts.

(2010) Domonic Brown hit .346 in 27 games earning a promotion to the big leagues after being promoted from Reading to AAA this summer ... Andy Tracy continued to produce, 21 HR & 80 RBI ... Michael Schwimer posted a 1.35 ERA, 16 H, 20 IP.

(2011) Brandon Moss had 23 home runs and 80 RBI, .275 average ... Michael Schwimer, 1.85 ERA, 47 games, 68 IP, 10 SV, 9-1 record.

(2012) Kevin Frandsen hit .302, 99 games … Cesar Hernandez made his AAA debut … Tyler Cloyd, 12-1, 2.35 ERA in 22 starts, 142 IP.

(2013) Cesar Hernandez hit .309, 104 games … Cody Asche hit a solid .295, 15 HR, 68 RBI … Mauricio Robles, 1.42 ERA, 34 G, 38 IP, 7 SV.

(2014) Maikel Franco, 16 HR, 78 RBI, 133 G, .275 … Ken Giles, 5 SV, 11 G before being promoted to the show.

(2015) Brian Bogusevic, .296,12 HR 57 RBI … Aaron Nola, 3-1, 6 GS, 3.58 ERA, 32.2 IP before being summoned to the big leagues … Maikel Franco, 33 G before he was called up to the bigs.

(2016) Darin Ruf, .294, 20 HR, 65 RBI … Jake Thompson, 11-5, 2.50, 21 GS, 129.2 IP.

(2017) Scott Kingery, .294, 63 G after being promoted from Reading … Dylan Cozen, 27 HR, 75 RBI despite hitting .210 … Tom Eshelman, 10-3, 2.23 ERA, 18 GS, 121 IP.

(2018) Joey Meneses had an incredible season, led IL with 23 HR, 82 RBI while second in hitting, .311 … Cole Irvin, 14-4, 2.57 ERA, 26 G, 161.1 IP … Enyel De Los Santos, 2.63 ERA, 22 GS, 126.2 IP.

(2019) Ali Castillo hit .316, third best IL … Nick Williams, .316, 48 G, 10 HR … Deivy Grullon, 21 HR, 77 RB, .283 … Austin Listi, after promotion from Reading, .278, 12 HR, 50 RBI … Austin Davis, 4-1, 2.75 ERA, 37 G, 52.1 IP.

Players of Note
JA Happ, Andy Tracy, Lou Marson, John Mayberry, Kyle Kendrick, Domonic Brown, Scott Mathieson, Freddy Galvis, Kevin Frandsen, Erik Kratz, Brandon Moss, Pete Orr, Justin De Fratus, Andres Blanco, Tyler Cloyd, Cody Asche, Cesar Hernandez, Michael Martinez, Tommy Joseph, Cameron Rupp, Adam Morgan, Michael Stutes, Maikel Franco, Hector Neris, David Buchanan, Ken Giles, Aaron Altherr, Brian Bogusevic, Darin Ruf, Jared Eickhoff, JP Crawford, Andrew Knapp, Ben Lively, Brock Stassi, Nick Williams, Jesmuel Valentin, Edward Mujica, Pedro Beato, Dylan Cozens, Jorge Alfaro, Rhys Hoskins, Scott Kingery, Cameron Perkins, Aaron Nola, Nick Pivetta, Roman Quinn, Tom Eshelman, Zach Eflin, Yacksel Rios, Luis Garcia, Dean Anna, Zach Green, Matt McBride, Ranger Suarez, Roman Quinn, Cole Irvin, Enyel De Los Santos, Deivy Grullon, Adam Haseley, Austin Davis, Edgar Garcia ...

Team Notes
(2011) Iron Pigs (80-64) lost Championship Series to Columbus Clippers, 3-1 ... (2016) Team posted their best regular season record (85-58 but lost the Championship Series to SWB.

■■■

Phillies AAA League MVP's
Pancho Herrera - 1959 - Buffalo - International League
Ted Savage - 1961 - Buffalo - International League
Ricardo Joseph - 1966 - San Diego - Pacific Coast League
Denny Doyle - 1969 - Eugene - Pacific Coast League
Shane Victorino - 2005 - Scranton Wilkes-Barre - International League

Rhys Hoskins - 2017 - Lehigh Valley - International League
Joey Meneses - 2018 - Lehigh Valley - International League

Phillies AAA League Pitchers of the Year
Brandon Duckworth - 2001 - Scranton Wilkes-Barre - International League
Joe Roa - 2002 - Scranton Wilkes-Barre - International League
Justin Lehr - 2009 - Lehigh Valley - also with Louisville - International League
Tyler Cloyd - 2012 - Lehigh Valley - International League
Jake Thompson - 2016 - Lehigh Valley - International League
Cole Irvin - 2018 - Lehigh Valley - International League

Phillies AAA Managers of the Year
Andy Seminick - 1972 - Eugene - Pacific Coast League
John Felske - 1983 - Portland - Pacific Coast League
Lee Elia - 1992 - Scranton Wilkes-Barre - International League
Marc Bombard - 2002 - Scranton Wilkes-Barre - International League
John Russell - 2006 - Scranton Wilkes-Barre - International League
Gary Jones - 2018 - Lehigh Valley - International League

Coca-Cola Park 2007 construction – Cheryl Pursell

Coca-Cola Park – Iron Pigs game – Cheryl Pursell

Coca-Cola Park – Iron Pigs game – Cheryl Pursell

Coca-Cola Park – Iron Pigs game – Cheryl Pursell

Coca-Cola Park – Iron Pigs game – Cheryl Pursell

Double A Level

When the minor league classifications were adjusted in 1963 to create the outline of the current structure, three double-A leagues were formed, the Eastern, Southern, and Texas. Previously they existed under various classifications.

The Phillies had working agreements with three teams pre 1963 and three thereafter. Their agreement with Reading which began in 1967 is the longest in AA and AAA ball.

Chronology of Class AA Affiliations
Baltimore, MD – International League – 1940
Tulsa, OK – Texas League – 1957-1958
Chattanooga, TN – Southern Association – 1960-1961
Chattanooga, TN – South Atlantic League – 1963-1965
Macon, GA - Southern League – 1966
Reading, PA - Eastern League – 1967-Present

Baltimore Orioles
In 1940 the Phillies had a one-year AA with the Baltimore Orioles of the International League, then a Class AA league. It was the highest level of eight Phillies minor league teams that year. Half were Class D, lowest level of that era.

They would return 11 years later to Baltimore when the League was bumped up to the AAA level.

Ballpark
Oriole Park V, also known as Terrapin Park. Built in 1914 to house Baltimore's Federal League team. Other new parks in the league were constructed of concrete and steel to guard against the fires that consumed many ballparks, but Terrapin Park was built of wood. The park burned on July 4, 1944, as a result of a fireworks mishap.

Manager
Tommy Thomas.

Team Notes
Defeated the Rochester Red Wings in the playoffs, 4-2; lost to the Championship Series to the Newark Bears, 4-3.

Tulsa Oilers

Professional baseball came to Tulsa, OK, in the form of the Oilers franchise in 1905 as an independent team in the Missouri Valley League. The Oilers joined the Texas League in 1933. The Phillies had a two-year affiliation from 1957-58.

Ballpark
Texas League Park was built in 1934 on the Tulsa County Fairgrounds. It was in operation through the 1980 season, after which it was demolished.

Managers
Al Widmar (1957-58), Jim Fanning (1958).

Climbing the Ladder
(1957) Roster average 28.4 years of age, oldest in the Phillies minor league system that season ... OF Jim Frey, 26, was the league's Player of The Year after leading in hits (198), runs (102), doubles (50), triples (11), stolen bases (21) and total bases (298). He was third in batting average (.336). His post-playing career included coaching and managing in the majors ... Widmar was a pitcher-manager both his years. He was the Phillies pitching coach, 1962-64; 1968-69.

Chattanooga Lookouts

For five seasons in a period of six years, Chattanooga, TN, was home to the Phillies AA minor league affiliate. The first two years (1960-61) the club was in the Southern Association which disbanded in 1962 leaving Chattanooga without a minor league team. With the reorganization of the minors in 1963, Chattanooga was awarded a franchise in the South Atlantic League with the understanding that the roster would include black athletes, a first in that city. Three Phillies ... OF Adolfo Phillips, OF Bobby Gene Sanders, and 1B Hank Allen were the first black athletes.

The team name Lookouts derives from Lookout Mountain. Its ridge spans three states: Alabama, Georgia, and Tennessee.

The franchise folded in 1966 and the Phillies moved their AA club to Macon, GA.

Ballpark

Engel Stadium. Constructed in 1930. Named after then team owner Joe Engel, a major league pitcher and longtime scout for the Washington Senators.

In 2012 Engel Stadium was used as the movie set for "42" - the life story of Jackie Robinson, the stadium was declared a historic landmark in 2014.

Managers

Spooks Jacobs (1960), Frank Lucchesi (1961) Jack Phillips (1963), Andy Seminick (1964-65).

Climbing the Ladder
(1963) Hank Allen, Adolfo Phillips, C Pat Corrales. (1964) LHP Grant Jackson, RHP Ferguson Jenkins, LHP Marcelino Lopez, RHP Bill Wilson, SS Mike Marshall.

Team Notes
(1961) Crowned league champions after 90-62 season.

Macon Peaches
Macon, GA, has a long history of baseball dating to 1892. First major league affiliation, 1929, with the Brooklyn Dodgers. Phillies had a one-year agreement in 1966 before moving to Reading, PA, the next year.

Ballpark
Luther Williams Field. Opened in 1929 and named after Macon's mayor. The original grandstand remains in place making it one of the oldest active ballparks. It is on the National Register of Historic Places.

Jackie Robinson broke the Georgia color barrier on April 7th, 1949 when he played for the Brooklyn Dodgers in an exhibition game at the stadium. It was also the location shooting for the 1976 film "The Bingo Long Traveling All Stars" and two 2012 films - "42" - chronicling legend Jackie Robinson and Clint Eastwood's film "Trouble with the Curve". The NetFlix series "Brockmire" also used the venue.

Manager
Andy Seminick.

Climbing the Ladder

Of the 29 players, 14 eventually reached the majors. Only one had a career over three years, RHP Jackie Brown who spent seven years in the majors with four different clubs but not the Phillies.

Eastern League logo, sportslogos.net

Texas League logo: sportslogos.net

Chattanooga, TN, Engle Field: ballparkreviews.com

Macon, GA, Luther Williams Field: ballparkreviews.com (entrance)

Macon, GA, Luther Williams Field: ballparkreviews.com (field)

Reading Fightin Phils

Reading's long history of organized baseball dates to 1858 when the Reading Athletic Club was formed. The Reading Actives were part of the Interstate League in 1883, the same year the Phillies were established in the National League.

Over the course of time, Reading's teams were known as the Actives, Coal Heavers, Pretzels, Coal Barons, Marines, Aces, Keystones, Chicks, Brooks, Indians (affiliation 1952-61; 1965), and Red Sox (affiliation 1933-34; 1963-64).

Cleveland's working agreement expired after the 1965 season, and Reading was without pro baseball for one year. Reading was awarded an Eastern League expansion franchise in 1967, and the long affiliation marriage with the Phillies began. Reading and the Phillies are tied with the

Detroit Tigers affiliation in Lakeland as the longest agreement in minor league baseball.

From 1967 through 2012 they were the Reading Phillies. Since 2013, the Fightin Phils.

Reading is also known as Baseballtown USA.

Ballpark

First Energy Stadium was built in 1951, and originally named Municipal Stadium in honor of the servicemen and women who gave their lives for the country. It underwent multiple upgrades over years, including a 10 million dollar renovation it 2011.

The ballpark is the first American baseball stadium to reach a total attendance of 10 million without ever serving as a team higher than the AA.

The ambiance of the ballpark and its historical depictions of the various teams are found in the concourse under the grandstand. An epic display. The grilled hot dogs served there are some of the best ballpark food that can be found.

Managers

Frank Lucchesi (1967-68), Bob Wellman (1969, 1974-76), Andy Seminick (1970), Nolan Campbell (1971), Jim Bunning (1972), Cal Emery (1973), Granny Hamner (1976), Lee Elia (1977-78), Jim Snyder (1979).

Ron Clark (1980-81), John Felske (1982), Bill Dancy (1983-84,1988,1994-95), Tony Taylor (1985), George Culver (1986-

87), Mike Hart (1989), Don McCormack (1990-93), Bill Robinson (1996), Al Leboeuf (1997-98).

Gary Varsho (1999-01), Greg Legg (2002-04, 2017-18), Steve Swisher (2005), PJ Forbes (2006-08), Steve Roadcap (2009-10), Mark Parent (2011), Dusty Wathan (2012-16), Shawn Williams (2019).

Climbing the Ladder
(1967) Club offensive leaders: OF Howie Bedell, hitting (.296) and RBI (66); 1B Jim Campbell, home runs (9), OF James Perkins, stolen bases (29) ... Pitching: RH Al Raffo, wins (12-6), ERA (2.22), strikeouts (104) ... 14 players reached the majors. SS Larry Bowa had the longest career (16 seasons); played 22 games AA debut.

Historical Nugget: Two pitchers on the staff were 40-year-old Robin Roberts and Dallas Green, 32; for each, it was their final season as a player ... "Robbie" was 5-3 with a 2.53 ERA. When no major league offers came along, he retired in June. Oddly his pro career began with 11 starts with the Wilmington Blue Rocks (1948) and ended after 11 starts in Reading, his only minor league seasons. ... Green finished 6-2, 1.77 for 8 starts. His pro career began with the Class D Mattoon Phillies (1955). After 8 starts there, he moved up to Class B (Reidsville Phillies) in the same season.

(1968) SS Larry Bowa, 2B Denny Doyle.

(1969) Ron Allen, younger brother of Dick Allen, 25 HR, 97 RBI, .300 ... LHP Ken Reynolds.

(1970) Greg Luzinski, 19, 33 HR, 120 RBI, .320; OPS.

(1971) Mike Schmidt made his pro debut on June 17. Playing shortstop for the major league Phillies in an exhibition game against the Reading Phillies; delivered a game-winning home run against Reading. Finished the season at .211, 8 HR, 34 RBI; played 74 games at SS ... Bob Boone played 3B ... 1B Andre Thornton, led club with 26 HR.

(1973) C John Stearns, #1 draft pick make pro debut ... OF Jerry Martin, 17 HR, 84 RBI, .300.

(1974) C Bill Nahorodny led club, 19 HR, 77 RBI ... RHP Roy Thomas, Tommy Underwood.

(1975) OF Rick Bosetti, 43 SB ... LHPs Willie Hernandez, Randy Lerch.

(1976) RHP Jim Wright, RHP Warren Brusstar.

(1977) C Keith Moreland.

(1978) RHP Dickie Noles, LHP Carlos Arroyo.

(1979) OF George Vukovich led club 13 HR, 88 RBI; .293 ... RHP Bob Walk; both on Phillies World Champions next season.

(1980) OF Bob Dernier, 71 SB ... SS Ryne Sandberg, 21 2B, 12 3B, 11 HR, 32 SB, .310 ... C Ozzie Virgil, led club 28 HR, 104 RBI ... LHP Mark Davis, pitching "Triple Crown", led EL in W (19-9), ERA (2.47), SO (185).

(1981) SS Julio Franco, OF Alejandro Sanchez, ... LHP Don Carman.

(1982) SS Steve Jeltz, C John Russell, C Jerry Willard, RHP Kevin Gross.

(1983) C Darren Daulton, 2B Juan Samuel, Jeff Stone, 90 SB ... Future Reading manager, INF Greg Legg, .306.

(1984) OF Chris James, C Mike LaValliere.

(1986) RHP Marvin Freeman, RHP Todd Frohwirth, RHP Mike Jackson, LHP Wally Ritchie, LHP Bruce Ruffin who took Steve Carlton's place in the rotation later that season after Lefty was released.

(1987) 1B Ricky Jordan, big-league debut next season.

(1989) SS Mickey Morandini began first pro season in Spartanburg, Clearwater, and then Reading; later returned as a coach ... RHP Jason Grimsley.

(1990) INF Kim Batiste, RHP Andy Ashby.

(1991) RHP Mike Williams.

(1992) C Mike Lieberthal, C Todd Pratt, SS Kevin Stocker.

(1994) C Gary Bennett ... RHP Rick Bottalico, ... Rehab appearances: John Kruk, Tommy Greene, Curt Schilling, Larry Andersen.

(1995) 2B David Doster, INF Kevin Sefcik, OF Wendell Magee ... RHP Mike Grace, RHP Wayne Gomes ... Larry Andersen, pitching coach.

(1996) C Bobby Estalella, 3B Scott Rolen, promoted to AAA and majors.

(1997) 2B Marlon Andersen.

(1998) LHP Randy Wolf.

(1999) 1B Pat Burrell, 28 HR, 90 RBI, .333; SS Jimmy Rollins, 21 2B, 8 3B, 11 HR, 56 RBI, 24 SB, .273.

(2000) OF Jason Michaels, C Johnny Estrada; SS Nick Punto, club-high 33 SB; OF Eric Valent, INF-OF Pete Rose Jr., 30 years old ... RHP Brandon Duckworth.

(2001) OF Marlon Byrd ... RHP Brett Myers, RHP Carlos Silva, RHP Geoff Geary.

(2002) RHP Ryan Madson.

(2004) 1B Ryan Howard, 37 HR, 102 RBI, .297; C Carlos Ruiz.

(2006) OF Michael Bourn ... LHP Geo Gonzalez, LHP J.A. Happ.

(2007) RHP Carlos Carrasco, RHP Kyle Kendrick.

(2008) INF Jason Donald, C Lou Marson, Carrasco; all three went to Cleveland in a trade for Cliff Lee, 7/29/2009.

(2009) OF Quintin Berry … RHP Kyle Drabek, LHP Joe Savery, RHP Vance Worley, LHP Mike Zagurski.

(2010) RHP Phillippe Aumont, RHP Justin DeFratus, RHP J.C. Ramirez.

(2011) SS Freddy Galvis … LHP Jake Diekman.

(2012) 3B Cody Asche, 2B Cesar Hernandez, 1B Tommy Joseph; big season for OF Darin Ruf, 32 2B, 38 HR, 104 RBI, .317 … RHP Jonathan Pettibone, RHP Trevor May.

(2013) 3B Maikel Franco, C Cameron Rupp … LHP Jesse Biddle, RHP Hector.

(2014) OF Aaron Altherr, OF Cameron Perkins … RHP Severino Gonzalez, LHP Hoby Milner, RHP Ken Giles, RHP Colton Murray.

(2015) C Andrew Knapp, OF Roman Quinn; 1B Brock Stassi, EL MVP, 15 HR, 90 RBI, .300 … RHP Zach Eflin, RHP Mark Leiter Jr., RHP Ben Lively, RHP Aaron Nola, RHP Nick Pivetta, RHP Jake Thompson.

(2016) The year of the Bash Brothers: OF Dylan Cozens, 38, 2B, 40 HR, 125 RBI, 1B Rhys Hoskins, 26 2B, 38 HR, 226 RBI, .281; C Jorge Alfaro, SS J.P. Crawford, RHP Victor Arano.

(2017) 2B Scott Kingery before promotion to AAA; 3B Mitch Walding … RHP Drew Anderson, LHP Austin Davis, LHP Cole Irvin, RHP Yacksel Rios.

(2018) C Deivi Grullon, OF Adam Haseley … Staff: RH Seranthony Dominquez, RH Edgar Garcia, LH JoJo Romero, LH Ranger Suarez.

(2019) 3B Alex Bohm … RHP Spencer Howard, RHP Connor Brogdon, RHP Ramon Rosso, RHP J.D. Hammer.

Team Notes
Championship Teams
(1968) Defeated Pittsfield, 3-1 … (1973) Defeated Pittsfield, 3-1 … (1995) Defeated New Haven, 3-2 … (2001) Declared co-champions due to stoppage of league play.

....

Eastern League MVP Award
Greg Luzinski - 1970
Mark Davis - 1980
Jeff Stone - 1983
Marlon Byrd - 2001
Ryan Howard - 2004
Darin Ruf - 2012
Brock Stassi - 2015
Dylan Cozens - 2016

....

EL Pitcher of the Year (Award began in 1995)
Ryan Madson - 2002

....

EL Rookie of the Year
Pat Burrell - 1999
Marlon Byrd - 2001
Ryan Howard - 2004
Chris Roberson - 2005

Michael Taylor - 2009
Darin Ruf - 2012
Rhys Hoskins - 2016

....

Manager of the Year
Bob Wellman - 1975
Lee Elia - 1978
Bill Dancy - 1983 & 1995
Al LeBeouf - 1997
Gary Varsho - 2000
Dusty Wathan - 2015 & 2016

....

Batting Champions
Bob Kelly - 1969 - .323
Greg Luzinski - 1970 - .325
Jim Olander - 1986 - .325
Randy Ruiz - 2005 - .349
Tagg Bozied - 2010 - .315

....

Home Runs Kings
Willie Darkis - 1983 - 31
Fred McNair - 1995 - 23
Jeff Inglin - 2003 – 24
Ryan Howard -2004 – 37
Darin Ruf - 2012 - 38
Jim Murphy - 2013 - 23
Dylan Cozens - 2016 – 40

....

Total Bases Leaders
Greg Luzinski - 1970 - 287
David Doster - 1995 - 254
Darin Ruf - 2012 - 303
Dylan Cozen - 2016 - 308

Darrick Hall - 2019 - 207

....

ERA Leaders
Bob Terlecki - 1971 - 2.30
Bob Walk - 1979 - 2.24
Mark Davis - 1980 - 2.47
Jay Baller - 1982 - 2.68
Gavin Floyd - 2004 - 2.57

....

Strikeout Leaders
Ken Reynolds - 1969 - 180
Roy Thomas - 1974 - 168
Bob Walk - 1970 - 135
Mark Davis - 1980 - 185
Brandon Duckworth - 2000 - 178
Austin Hyatt - 2011 – 171

....

Reading, PA, 1967 logo: sportslogos.net

1950's view – Municipal Stadium – courtesy of Reading Eagle

2019 View - First Energy Stadium – photo by George Youngs Jr

First Energy Stadium – Michael Dill

First Energy Stadium – Michael Dill

Reading Municipal Stadium – Charles O'Reilly

Reading Municipal Stadium – Charles O'Reilly

Reading game action – photo by George Youngs Jr

Reading concourse inside stadium – George Youngs Jr

Best Hot Dog in the Minors – Photo by George Youngs Jr

Reading game action – Photo by George Youngs Jr

Photo by George Youngs Jr

Photo by George Youngs Jr

Photo by George Youngs Jr

Single A Level

The Phillies have had player development contracts with 21 cities in the Class A division. That includes some cities designated as such before the 1963 minor league realignment. Over time the division was split even further into "Advanced A" and "A" which is sometimes referred to as "Low A".

Here is a list of the Class A cities in which the Phillies have had or continue to have player development agreements. According to baseball-reference.com, Clearwater became an Advanced A affiliation in 1990. All others until then and since are considered as A level affiliations.

Chronology of Class A Affiliations
Hazelton, PA – New York Penn League – 1934-1936
Utica, NY – Eastern League – 1943-1950
Schenectady, NY – Eastern League – 1951-1957
Tri-Cities, WA - Western International League – 1952
Spokane, WA - Western International League – 1953
Salem, OR - Western International League – 1954
Williamsport, PA – Eastern League – 1958-1962
Asheville, NC – South Atlantic League – 1959-1960
Miami, FL – Florida State League – 1963-1965
Spartanburg, SC – South Atlantic League – 1963-1994
Twin Falls, ID – Pioneer League – 1963
Bakersfield, CA – California League – 1963-1967
Eugene, OR – Northwest League – 1964-1965
Portsmouth, VA – Carolina League – 1966-1968
Raleigh-Durham, NC – Carolina League – 1969
Hampton, VA – Carolina League – 1970-1971
Rocky Mount, NC – Carolina League – 1973-1975
Newport News, VA – Carolina League – 1976-1985
Clearwater, FL – Florida State League – 1985 – Present

Kannapolis, NC – South Atlantic League – 1995-2000
Lakewood, NJ – South Atlantic League – 2001-Present

Utica Blue Sox

The Utica Braves began play in 1939 when Ambrose
McConnell purchased the Auburn Bouleys franchise in the
Class C Can-Am League and moved the club to Utica. The
Phillies entered into a player development contract from
1943-50. Utica moved to the class A Eastern League and in
1944 the club was renamed the Blue Sox.

Ballpark

Ambrose McConnell Field. The ballpark was built in 1937 and
was originally named Braves Field. It was the innovation of
one-time major leaguer and owner Ambrose McConnell.
When he died in 1942, the field was renamed after him.
The park was demolished in the 1950s to make a New York
State Thruway Exit.

Managers

Wally Schang (1943), Eddie Sawyer (1944-47), Dick Porter
(1948), Pat Colgan (1948-49), Lee Riley (1950).

Climbing the Ladder

(1945) Richie Ashburn, SS Granny Hamner, INF Putsy
Caballero; (1947) Stan Lopata; (1948) 3B Willie Jones, OF
Jackie Mayo; (1949) RHP Steve Ridzik; (1950). All played for
the 1950 National League champion Phillies.

Team Notes

(1945) Ashburn, 18, made his pro debut and posted a .312
batting average. Manager Eddie Sawyer converted him from

a catcher to center fielder to take advantage of his speed ... (1947) After serving in the military Ashburn, 20, returned to Utica and hit .362, second in the league.; led the league with 194 hits. That team defeated the Wilkes-Barre Barons in the Championship Series, 4-2.

Schenectady Blue Jays

After spending five seasons (1946-50) in the Class C Canadian-American League, the Schenectady Blue Jays moved up to the Class A Eastern League in 1951. The Phillies remained through 1957.

Ballpark

McNearney Stadium. The ballpark was known for bright field lights, a contribution from the General Electric Company which was headquartered in Schenectady at the time. The same lighting system was eventually installed in Yankee Stadium. When pro baseball departed, the stadium site became part of the Stadium Golf Club.

Managers

Lee Riley (1951), Danny Carnevale (1952), Skeeter Newsome (1953), Lew Krause, Snuffy Stirnweiss (1954), Don Osborne (1955), Dick Carter (1956-1957).

Climbing the Ladder

(1951) OF Mel Clark, RHP Jack Sanford; (1952) INF Ted Kazanski; (1953) OF Bob Bowman, RHP Dick Farrell, RHP Jack Meyer; (1954) LHP Seth Morehead; (1955) 1B Ed Bouchee, RHP Don Cardwell; (1956) OF Chuck Essegian.

Team Notes
(1955) Lost to Allentown Cardinals in the playoffs ... (1956) After posting league-best 84-54 record, swept Reading Indians in the Championship Series.

Tri-City Braves
The Tri-Cities (Kennewick, Richland, and Pasco) are in southeastern Washington state. The Tri-City Braves were a member of the Western International League (1950-54), then became a charter member of the new Northwest League in 1955. Phillies were there in 1952.

Ballpark
Sanders-Jacobs Field (Kennewick). Home to seven different minor league organizations (1950-75). Demolished after 1975 season.

Manager
Charlie Gassaway.

Spokane Indians
Spokane's minor league history dates to 1892 (Pacific Northwest League). In 1937, Spokane became a charter member of the Western International League, predecessor of the Northwest League. The Phillies were there in 1953.

Ballpark
Ferris Field. Named for city attorney George M. Ferris, former player and manager for the Indians. The wooden grandstand was built in 1936.

Manager
Don Osborne.

Salem Senators
The Senators team was founded in 1940. A later incarnation started in 1977 and remains in the Northwest League as the Hillsboro Hops. Another one year stay for the Phillies (1954).

Ballpark
George E Waters Field. Named for the original owner of the Salem Senators. In 1976, a US Post Office facility was built and continues to occupy the former site of Waters Field.

Managers
Harvey Storey, Hal Lubey.

Williamsport Grays
The Williamsport Grays were a charter member of the New York–Pennsylvania League established in 1923 and later became the Eastern League in 1938. The Phillies were the last affiliate of the Grays (1958-62).

Ballpark
Bowman Field was completed in 1926. During its first three years, it was known as Memorial Field because of its location inside of the surrounding park. By 1929, the Grays club officials deemed it appropriate to name the field "Bowman Field" in honor of Gray's club president, J. Walton Bowman, who had been the main force in raising the money to build the facility.

Managers
Dick Carter (1958), Frank Lucchesi (1959-60,1962), Andy Seminick (1961).

Climbing the Ladder
(1958) RHP Art Mahaffey; (1959) SS Bobby Wine; (1960) INF-OF Danny Cater, INF Lee Elia, OF John Herrnstein, OF Ted Savage, RHP Dwight Siebler; (1961) RHP Ray Culp, LHP Marcelino Lopez, RHP Jack Hamilton; (1962) OF Dick Allen, C Pat Corrales.

Team Notes
Allen's third pro season, .329, 20 home runs, 109 RBI; led league in doubles (32), OBP (.409), OPS (.957) ... the Grays lost in the Championship Series (1959, 1962); declared co-champs with the Springfield Giants (1960) when rain halted the series after one game.

Asheville Tourists
Professional baseball in Asheville initially began in 1897 and has been played continuously for nearly every year since 1909. The "Tourists" name began in 1915 when local sportswriters began referring to the team as such.

Asheville has been in 14 different minor leagues and five classifications (B, C, D, A, and AA). They were part of the fourth version of the Class A South Atlantic League when the Phillies fielded teams (1959-60).

Ballpark
McCormick Field. Built in 1924, it is one of the oldest minor-league stadiums still in regular use.

Managers
Clyde McCullough (1959), Chuck Kress (1960).

Climbing the Ladder
(1960) LHP Dennis Bennett, RHP Ray Culp.

Miami Marlins

After a three-year run as a AAA affiliate in the International League (1956-58), the Phillies returned to Miami, FL, (1962-65) in a lower classification. The Florida State League was known as a D League in 1962 but became an Advanced A level when minor league baseball did its full-scale reclassifications in 1963.

Under the new classifications, the Phillies of 1963 consisted of four Class A teams: Miami, Bakersfield, CA; Spartanburg, SC, and Magic Valley [Twins Falls, ID], AA Chattanooga, TN, and AAA Arkansas [Little Rock].

Ballpark
Miami Stadium. It served as the spring training home of the Brooklyn and LA Dodgers (1950-58) and the Baltimore Orioles (1959-90). Built in 1949, it was demolished 50 years later.

Managers
Andy Seminick (1962-63), Bobby Morgan (1964-65).

Climbing the Ladder
(1962) RHP Ferguson Jenkins, OF Alex Johnson. (1963) 1B-OF Hank Allen. (1964) OF Joe Lis. Pro debuts for Jenkins, Johnson, Lis.

Spartanburg Phillies

For the longest time, the longest-tenured Phillies minor league club was in Spartanburg, SC. How long? 22 years, 1963-1994.

In 1963, the Spartanburg Phillies were born as an A level member of the Western Carolinas League, then switched to the South Atlantic League concurrent with the league's 1980 name change. The Spartanburg franchise also changed its name to the Traders (1980), Spinners (1983), and Suns (1984) before reverting to the Phillies in 1986.

The franchise moved to Kannapolis, NC, following the 1994 season.

Ballpark

Duncan Park. Originally opened in 1926. Eighty years later it was listed on the National Register of Historic Places.

Following the closing of Connie Mack Stadium in 1970, some 500 seats were shipped to Duncan Park.

Managers

Lou Kahn (1963), Dick Teed (1964; 1967), Moose Johnson (1965), Bob Wellman (1966; 1971-1972), Bobby Malkmus (1968-1969), Howie Bedell (1970; 1973-1974), Lee Elia (1975-1976), Mike Compton (1977), Ron Clark (1978), Bill Dancy (1979), Tom Harmon (1980-1981), Tony Taylor (1982), P.J. Carey (1982), Roly de Armas (1983; 1985-1986), Jay Ward (1984), Ramon Aviles (1987), Mel Roberts (1988-1989; 1991), Rick Colbert (1990), Roy Majtyka (1992-1994).

Titles

Spartanburg won the WCL titles in 1966, 1967, 1972, 1973, 1975, and the 1988 SAL championship. Twice, Spartanburg lost in the championship playoffs, 1968 and 1979.

Manager Bob Wellman's 1966 team was ranked #78 in the top 100 minor league teams of all time as selected by the National Association in 2001. That club finished 91-35. Between July 17 and August 12, the Phillies won 25 in a row. The streak included 20 complete games and just 17.1 innings from the bullpen.

Climbing the Ladder

Pitchers

LH Ken Reynolds, RH Barry Lersch, LH Mike Wallace, RH Roy Thomas, LH Tom Underwood, RH Warren Brusstar, LH Willie Hernandez, LH Kevin Saucier, RH Jim Wright, RH Dickie Noles, RH Marty Bystrom, RH Bob Walk, RH Jerry Reed, LH Don Carman, LH Mark Davis, RH Jay Baller, RH Kelly Downs, RH Kevin Gross, RH Mike Maddux, RH Lance McCullers, RH Michael Jackson, RH Bob Scanlan, RH Scott Service, RH Andy Ashby, RH Jason Grimsley, LH Chuck McElroy, RH Toby Borland, RH Bob Wells, RH Ricky Bottalico, RH Mike Grace.

Catchers

Larry Cox, Buck Martinez, Jim Essian, Keith Moreland, Ozzie Virgil, Darren Daulton, Mike LaValliere, Mike Lieberthal, Gary Bennett, Bobby Estalella.

Infielders

Larry Bowa, Denny Doyle, John Vukovich, Andre Thornton, Manny Trillo, Jim Morrison, Luis Aguayo, Greg Walker, Ryne Sandberg, Steve Jeltz, Francisco Melendez, Juan Samuel, Rick Schu, Ricky Jordan, Kim Batiste, Mickey Morandini, Kevin Stocker, Scott Rolen.

Outfielders

Jerry Martin, Rick Bosetti, Lonnie Smith, Bob Dernier, George Bell, Jeff Stone, Chris James, Rick Parker.

Team Notes

Dancy, de Armas, Roberts, Carey all played in Spartanburg and wound up managing there. Arroyo pitched there and is still active in the Phillies' player development. Dave Wallace had a short major league career as a pitcher but a long career as a pitching coach in the show.

Pat Williams, a young protégé of maverick promoter Bill Veeck, ran constant promotions that packed Duncan Park in the 1960s. Attendance in 1966 set a single-A record, 173,010. Williams, once a catcher in the Phillies minor league system, went on to a very successful career as an executive of several NBA teams.

Photo by Marc Viquez

Shibe Park seats still exist

By Marc Viquez

It is one of the oldest baseball stadiums in the country and the oldest in South Carolina. The place looks old as you approach its grandstands and eventually walk through its entrance. It has seen various baseball stars throughout its 94-year history and recently received a much-needed upgrade. Its biggest asset is the original chairs from Shibe Park in Philadelphia; there aren't many places like Duncan Park Stadium in Spartanburg, SC.

However, how did seats that predate the ballpark by a little over two decades wind up in Spartanburg in the first place? That question is very easy to answer; they were hauled in by truck from Philadelphia and placed here when the Phillies operated a minor league club in town.

The seats were installed in Shibe Park (later Connie Mack Stadium) in 1909 but when the Phils won their last game at the stadium on October 1, 1970, many in attendance stormed the field in an attempt to bring home a souvenir from the then 61-year-old ballpark. A story that ran by the Associated Press reported the following scene:

"Armed with hacksaws, crowbars, and hammers, most of the crowd of 31,822 tore up bases, tarpaulins, outfield signs, seats, broadcast booths, and anything that could be moved."

The game was an afterthought and even during the radio broadcast, you could hear the sounds of banging and cutting with many in attendance trying to pry away a seat or two to take home for a souvenir. The Phillies would win that game in extra innings over the Montreal Expos 2-1 and fans poured onto the field by the thousands. Fans walked off with rows of seats, bases, and other treasures of Shibe Park.

In August of 1971, a fire destroyed a majority of the stadium that was becoming an eyesore to the neighborhood. In 1976, the ballpark was razed during the Major League All-Star Festivities, ironically, at the city's new Veterans Stadium.

Fortunately, a selection of 587 seats was transferred 600 miles south to the Phillies' Single-A team in Spartanburg and installed in Duncan Park before the 1971 Western Carolinas League season; the only minor league ballpark to receive them. If these seats had remained at the abandoned stadium in Philadelphia, they would have been vandalized, stripped away by looters, burned, or destroyed by the wrecking ball.

The resurrected seats would continue to be part of the organization in Spartanburg until the team relocated after the 1994 season. Once again abandoned by the Phillies, the seats remained intact as college, amateur, and high school baseball would call the ballpark home. Today, it is home to both Spartanburg High School varsity and junior varsity and American Legion Post 28, baseball teams.

Lenny Mathis, President of Friends of Duncan Park, told me in 2013 that the wooden seats have not been used since the summer of 2005 and are blocked off from the contour plastic chairs that were installed in 1968. He also added that the ballpark itself has held up well due to its steel structure, concrete concourse, and roof.

This past year a total of $1.6 million was used towards renovations of the historic ballpark that were long overdue. The improvements included upgrades to the dugouts, a new outfield wall, strengthening the grandstand, removal of rust, and the addition of weather-resistant paint. The green plastic box seats were updated, and the old wooden benches were replaced, and a fresh coat of paint was added.

The original 1909 seats are separated by fencing along the concourse and are in pristine shape. The faded green and splintered, fold-down chairs feature an ornate butterfly design between their legs and should be given proper respect when sitting in them. The amount of Hall of Famers, World Series games, and future stars in the minor leagues have all been viewed from these historic chairs. Whoever thought of moving these seats elsewhere must have been a saint.

Duncan Park Stadium is a true original and one of a handful of ballparks that are still around from the 1920s. The much-needed renovations have the place looking brand new as it prepares to host high school and legion baseball in the spring and summer and pretty soon the old place will be celebrating a century of use. They truly don't make them like this anymore.

(Marc Viquez www.stadiumjourney.com June 9, 2020)

Magic Valley Cowboys

For three years the Phillies had minor league teams in Twin Falls, ID, the Magic Valley Cowboys (1961-63). In all three seasons, the team was in the Pioneer League. When baseball changed the classifications in 1963 to A, AA, and AAA, the league became Class A.

Originally the Twin Falls Cowboys, the club was renamed the Magic Valley Cowboys in 1952. Their last season in pro ball was 1971.

Ballpark
Jaycee Field. The ballpark was constructed during the spring of 1939, as a WPA project. The baseball field was adjacent to a four-acre public park named Harmon Park and later incorporated into an expanded Harmon Park.

Manager
Moose Johnson.

Climbing the Ladder
(1963) OF Alex Johnson, SS Mike Marshall.

Team Notes
(1963) Lost the Championship Series to the Idaho Falls Yankees, 2-0.

Bakersfield Bears
For 11 seasons, the Phillies had a minor league affiliate in Bakersfield, California, (1956; 1958-67). It was the longest relationship in that city's minor league history that began in 1946 and ended in 2016. Currently, Bakersfield is in the Pecos League, an independent league.

While the Phillies were there, the team was known as the Boosters (1956) and then the Bears the rest of the time. Initially a Class C team, the Bears became a Class A California League club in the new minor league structure in 1963.

Ballpark
Sam Lynn Ballpark. Built in 1941 by the WPA. The sun set over the 15-foot-high CF fence causing problems for batters, catchers and umpires. Day games didn't begin until after sunset. It remains in use today as home to the independent team.

Managers
Bob Wellman (1963), Moose Johnson (1964), Dick Teed (1965-66), Nolan Campbell (1967).

Climbing the Ladder
(1963) OF John Briggs, RHP Gary Wagner, RHP Rick Wise. (1964) RHP Jackie Brown, OF Joe Lis. (1966) RHP Billy Champion, SS Terry Harmon. (1967) SS Larry Bowa.

Eugene Emeralds

The Phillies and the Eugene (OR) Emeralds had a 10-year relationship in minor league baseball (1964-1973). During that time, Oregon's third-largest populous city was in three different minor league classifications. Games were played in two different ballparks. For two seasons (1964-1965) they played in the then Class A Northwest League (140-game schedule).

Ballpark

Bethel Park was one of the last wooden parks used in minor league baseball. It was built in 1949 in West Eugene. The stadium became home to the Emeralds (1955-58). After the 1968 season, it was torn down for what was initially expected to be part of a highway. Later Lark City Park was built on part of the old outfield.

Manager

Bob Wellman (1964-65), Hal Luby (1965).

Climbing the Ladder

(1964) LHP Grant Jackson, RHP Bill Wilson; (1965) SS Mike Marshall made a transition to pitching. Nine years later he would win the National League Cy Young Award while pitching for the Dodgers.

Tidewater Tides

For three seasons, Portsmouth, VA, was host to a Phillies minor league team in the Class A Carolina League (1966-68). The team was known as the Tidewater Tides.

Ballpark
Lawrence Stadium was built in 1941; served minor league baseball through the 1969 season. It was demolished in 1997.

Managers
Bobby Morgan, Lou Kahn (1966), Bob Wellman (1967-68).

Climbing the Ladder
(1966) RHP Barry Lersch. (1967) RHP Jackie Brown, RHP Billy Champion, C Larry Cox, 2B Denny Doyle, SS Terry Harmon, OF Larry Hisle, LHP Ken Reynolds. (1968) RHP Steve Arlin, OF Joe Lis, 3B John Vukovich, LHP Bill Laxton.

Raleigh-Durham Phillies
For one season (1969) the Phillies had a Class A minor league team in Durham, NC, a member of the Carolina League. The Phillies fielded a team in the Carolina League from 1966 through 1985 in four different communities.

Ballparks
The team had two home fields ... one in Raleigh and one in Durham.

Durham Athletic Park in Durham still exists and is the home field for the North Carolina Central University and the Durham School of the Arts baseball teams. The stadium was the primary setting for the movie Bull Durham.

Devereux Meadow Park in Raleigh was built in 1938 and remained in use till 1971. It was demolished in 1979 and turned into a parking lot for the city's sanitation department trucks. It's now targeted for parkland development.

Manager
Nolan Campbell.

Climbing the Ladder
3B Bob Boone, C Larry Cox, 1B Greg Luzinski.

Team Notes
Boone joined the club after being drafted from Stanford University. He played 79 games at third base and hit .300 … The 18-year-old Luzinski, in his second pro season, played 129 games and led the league in home runs (31), RBI (92), and total bases (255) … After winning the Eastern Division, the Phillies defeated the Burlington Senators, 2-1, to win the Championship.

Peninsula Phillies/Pilots
Twice the Phillies had a minor league team in Hampton, VA, in the Class A Carolina League. First, the Peninsula Phillies (1970-71) and later the Peninsula Pilots (1976-85).

Ballpark
War Memorial Stadium was built in 1947 and designed by Branch Rickey. It remains in use today as host to minor league baseball in the Carolina League.

Managers
Nolan Campbell (1970), Howie Bedell (1971), Cal Emery (1976), Jim Snyder (1977-78), Ron Clark (1979; 1984-85), Bill Dancy (1980-82), Tony Taylor (1983).

Climbing the Ladder
(1970) OF Mike Anderson, 1B Andre Thornton. (1971) 1B Bob Beall, C Jim Essian, LHP Mac Scarce. (1976) OF Bobby Brown, 1B Len Matuszek, C Keith Moreland, LHP Kevin Saucier. (1977) INF Luis Aguayo, RHP Dickie Noles, RHP Bob Walk. (1978) C Ozzie Virgil, OF George Vukovich, RHP Marty Bystrom, RHP Jerry Reed. (1979) OF Bobby Dernier, 1B Greg Walker. (1980) SS Julio Franco, RHP Roy Smith, LHP Don Carman, RHP Warren Brusstar. (1981) 1B Francisco Melendez, C Jerry Willard, RHP Jay Baller, RHP Kelly Downs. (1982) C Darren Daulton, 2B Juan Samuel, OF Jeff Stone, C Mike LaValliere, RHP Charles Hudson. (1983) 3B Rick Schu, RHP Mike Maddux. (1985) RHP Todd Frohwirth, RHP Michael Jackson.

Team Notes
(1982) Stone stole a whopping 94 bases! ... Hudson went 15-5; promoted to big leagues the next season ... Juan Samuel led the league in total bases (283) and hit .320 with 29 home runs and 64 stolen bases.

Titles
Won seven Carolina League Division Championships and made six trips to the Carolina League Championship Series.

(1971) Won Championship Series over Kinston Eagles, 2-0 ... (1977) Won Championship Series over Lynchburg Mets, 3-2 ... (1978) Lost Championship Series to Lynchburg Mets, 3-0 ... (1980) After a 100-40 record in the regular season, won their playoff series over the Durham Bulls, 3-1 but lost the Championship Series to the Hagerstown Suns, 3-0 ...

The 1980 team had a .714 winning percentage, which was the best in Carolina League history. It still stands as one of the top 20 all-time records in professional baseball history.

Rocky Mount Phillies

Sandwiched between two stints in Hampton, VA, the Phillies spent three seasons in Rocky Mount, NC (1973-75). The team was still the Carolina League.

Ballpark
Municipal Stadium Park dates to 1915. The grandstand was torn down in 1987, but the baseball field remains. It is now called Rocky Mt. Municipal Stadium.

Managers
Bob Wellman (1973), Cal Emery (1974-75).

Climbing the Ladder
(1973) C Bill Nahorodny, INF Greg Prior, RHP Roy Thomas. (1974). RHP Dan Boitano, OF Rick Bosetti, SS Todd Cruz, LHP Randy Lerch, 3B Jim Morrison, C John Stearns. (1975) Warren Brusstar.

Team Notes
(1975) Rocky Mount Phillies won the championship in the four-team league, 91-51, 10.5 games ahead of the Winston-Salem Red Sox. With four teams, the league didn't have a Championship Series.

Thomas, 20, shared the CL high in wins (15-8) and strikeouts (193). He was the Phillies first-round selection in 1971 ... Stearns, 22, led the league in hitting (.343). He was also a first-rounder in 1974 ... Brusstar, a solid reliever on the

1980 World Champion Phillies, was a starter in A ball. The 23-year-old shared the CL high in wins (14-8) ... Two future Phillies minor league managers were on the same club, C Roly de Armas and C P.J. Carey.

Piedmont Phillies

Following 22 seasons in Spartanburg, SC, the Phillies Class A South Atlantic League affiliation was relocated to Kannapolis, NC, in 1995. The Phillies remained there through 2000 when they moved to Lakewood, NJ. The Chicago White Sox replaced the Phillies (Kannapolis Intimidators) and have been there since.

Ballpark

Fieldcrest Cannon Stadium. Originally built in 1994 by the Fieldcrest Cannon Corporation, a textile giant in the city.

Managers

Roy Majtka (1995-96), Ken Oberkfell (1997-99), Greg Legg (2000).

Climbing the Ladder

(1997) SS Jimmy Rollins, RHP Adam Eaton, (1998) C Johnny Estrada, OF Eric Valent, RHP Brandon Duckworth, (1999) RHP Carlos Silva, RHP Derrick Turnbow, (2000) OF Marlon Byrd, RHP Ryan Madson, RHP Brett Myers.

Team Notes

(1995) Won North Division (81-59); lost Championship Series to Augusta GreenJackets . . . (2000) Won North Division (90-47); lost Championship Series to Augusta GreenJackets.

Asheville, NC, McCormick Field: Charles O'Reilly

Spartanburg, SC, Duncan Park: Marc Viquez

Spartanburg, SC, Duncan Park: Marc Viquez

Durham, NC, Athletic Park: Charles O'Reilly

Hampton, VA, War Memorial Stadium: Charles O'Reilly

Rocky Mount, NC, Municipal Stadium Park: Charles O'Reilly

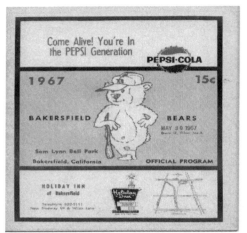

Bakersfield, CA, 1967 scorecard: californialeaguehistory.com

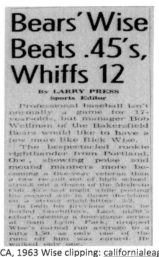

Bears' Wise Beats .45's, Whiffs 12

By LARRY PRESS
Sports Editor

Professional baseball isn't normally a game for 17-year-olds, but manager Bob Wellman of the Bakersfield Bears would like to have a few more like Rick Wise.

The bespectacled rookie righthander from Portland, Ore., showing poise and mound manners more becoming a five-year veteran than a raw recruit out of high school, struck out a dozen of the Modesto Colt .45's last night while posting his second win in three decisions on a strong eight-hitter 3-2.

In both his previous starts he hurled two-hitters. Last night's effort, opening a four-game series at Sam Lynn Park, dropped Wise's earned run average to a nifty 1.50 as only one of the runs off him was earned. He walked only one.

Bakersfield, CA, 1963 Wise clipping: californialeaguehistory.com

BAKERSFIELD BEARS BASEBALL TEAM 1963
(front center) Bill Hoffman, Bat Boy
(left to right-first row) Bill Wilson, LeRoy Thomas, Dave Ortwein, Jim Enold,
Jim Perkins, Dennis Van Cleve, Lou Garvin.
(second row) Ted Zipeto (trainer), Bob Wellman (manager), Sammy Martinez,
Jerry Messerly, Gary Wagner, Gary Curkendall.
(third row) Frank Rubino, Jim Couch, Gene Weston, John Briggs, Denny
Kennedy, Don Bridges.

Bakersfield, CA, 1963 Bears photo: californialeaguehistory.com

Bakersfield Bears
BASEBALL CLUB
Affiliated with the Philadelphia Phillies

BAKERSFIELD BASEBALL BOOSTERS, INC.

OFFICERS

BOB KING
President

WALLY BEARDSLEY
Vice President

BOB WILLIAMS
Secretary

FLOYD BURCHAM
Treasurer

MAYNARD BOMMER
Bus. Mgr.

RAY NEWMAN
Dir. of Advertising

DIRECTORS

DON BLACKMORE
JOHN BOYDSTUN
JACK BRIGGS
TONY CUETO
JOE GANNON
GALEN (TEX) GREER
RAY JARRARD
JOHN LINDLEY

ED MACKIGHT
TOM MILLOY
JOHN MIGLAS
JOHN NAIRN
CLEO POLLARD
KEN SHANNON

Bakersfield, CA, 1963 front office: californialeagehistory.com

199

Clearwater Phillies/Threshers

The Florida State League (FSL) was founded in 1919 and, except for two interruptions (1928-36 when the league closed, and 1942-45 WW II), it has played every year. It operated as a "Class D" league until 1963 when it was named an "A level" league as part of the minor league reorganization. In 1990, the league was designated as an "Advanced A" level of play.

Clearwater first had a team in the league in 1924 when the Daytona independent team franchise moved briefly over to Clearwater to play 21 games.

In 1985 the Phillies became an ongoing member of the FSL when they established a minor league team in Clearwater. They played as the Clearwater Phillies until the 2004 season when they became the Clearwater Threshers coinciding with the move from Jack Russell Stadium to what is now known as Spectrum Field.

Ballparks
Jack Russell Stadium opened in 1955 as the spring training home of the Phillies and the home of the Clearwater Phillies for 19 seasons.

Managers
Ramon Aviles (1985, 2001), Ron Clark (1986), Roly de Armas (1987, 2001-02,2004), Granny Hamner (1988), Glenn Gulliver (1989), Lee Elia (1990-91), Bill Dancy (1992-93, 1998-99), Don McCormack (1994-95), Al Leboeuf (1996), Roy Majtyka (1997), Ken Oberkfell (2000), John Morris (2002), Mike Schmidt (2004), Greg Legg (2005-06, 2015-16), Dave Huppert

(2007), Razor Shines (2008), Ernie Whitt (2009), Dusty Wathan (2010-11), Chris Truby (2012-13), Nelson Prada (2014), Shawn Williams (2017-18), Marty Malloy (2019).

Climbing the Ladder
(1985) 1B Ricky Jordan; (1986) OF Ron Jones; (1987) C Darren Daulton; (1989) IF Kim Batiste, 2B Mickey Morandini; (1991) C Mike Lieberthal; (1992) SS Kevin Stocker; (1993) C Gary Bennett, RHP Ricky Bottalico, RHP Wayne Gomes; (1995) 3B Scott Rolen; (1996) 2B Marlon Anderson; (1998) OF Pat Burrell, SS Jimmy Rollins, OF Eric Valent, RHP Brandon Duckworth; (1999) SS Anderson Machado, OF Jason Michaels, IF Nick Punto.

(2001) 3B Travis Chapman, 2B Chase Utley, RHP Ryan Madson; (2002) C Carlos Ruiz; (2003) 1B Ryan Howard, LHP Cole Hamels; (2004) RHP Alfredo Simon; (2005) RHP Kyle Kendrick; (2006) C Tuffy Gosewisch, LHP JA Happ; (2007) OF Domonic Brown, RHP Carlos Carrasco; (2009) SS Freddy Galvis; (2010) 1B Darin Ruf, LHP Jake Diekman, RHP Trevor May; (2011) 2B Cesar Hernandez; (2012) LHP Adam Morgan, RHP Hector Neris; (2013) OF Aaron Altherr, 3B Maikel Franco, C Tommy Joseph, RHP Ken Giles; (2014) SS JP Crawford, C Deivy Grullon, C Andrew Knapp, OF Roman Quinn, RHP Aaron Nola; (2015) C Willians Astudillo, 1B Rhys Hoskins, C Andrew Knapp, RHP Victor Arano; (2016) 3B Zach Green, 2B Scott Kingery; (2017) RHP Seranthony Dominguez, RHP JD Hammer, LHP Cole Irvin, LHP Ranger Suarez, RHP Jacob Waguespack; (2018) OF Adam Haseley, RHP Ramon Rosso, RHP Sixto Sanchez; (2019) 3B Alec Bohm, RHP Connor Brogdon, RHP Spencer Howard.

Team Notes

Championship Teams: (1993, 75-60 season) Defeated the St. Lucie Mets in the Finals, 3-1 ... (2007, 83-57) Defeated the Brevard County Manatees, 3-1.

Championship Finals: (1991, 81-49) Lost to the West Palm Beach Expos, 2-0...(1996, 75-62) Lost to the St Lucie Mets, 3-1

(2018) OF Jose Pujols was the first Clearwater player to win the "FSL Player of the Year" Award that was initiated in 2004.

Batting Champions
Ron Jones - 1985 - .371
Wendell Magee - 1995 - .353
Ryan Howard - 2003 - .303
Willians Astudillo - 2015 - .314
....

FSL Home Run Champions
Steve De Angelis - 1985 - 16
Jimmy Fortenberry - 1986 - 18
Dan Held - 1995 - 21
Ryan Howard - 2003 - 23
Andrew Pullin - 2015 - 14
....

FSL Pitching Strikeout Leaders
Rob Burger - 1997 - 154
Trevor May - 2011 - 208
Jesse Biddle - 2012 - 151
Mauricio Llovera - 2018 - 137
....

FSL ERA Leaders
Mark Rutherford - 1998 - 2.65
Miguel Ascencio - 2001 - 2.84
Josh Outman - 2007 - 2.45

Photo by Mark Wylie

Threshers Game Action – photo by Mark Wylie

Threshers Game Action – photo by Mark Wylie

Threshers Game Action – photo by Mark Wylie

Clearwater Baseball History

Athletic Field

Photo by Rich Westcott

Ground was broken for Athletic Field in December 1922. Cost of building the park was $25,000. It included a small clubhouse and a 2,000-seat wooden grandstand. Clearwater's population was about 3,000. Originally called Clearwater Athletic Field, it was renamed Ray Green Field in honor of Ray Green, Mayor of Clearwater (1935-1938), who was instrumental in upgrading the facility during his tenure.

Spring training: The Brooklyn Robins (Dodgers) were the first team (1923-1932; 1936-41). Between Brooklyn's two stints, the International League Newark Bears, (1933-35) trained there. The Cleveland Indians for two years (1942, 1946), followed by the Phillies (1947-54). Prior to moving to Clearwater, the Phillies trained in Miami Beach in 1946.

Season home: The Clearwater Pelicans (Florida State League, 1924), Clearwater Bombers (Amateur Softball Association (1945-54), and the Clearwater Black Sox (Negro Leagues) in 1952.

The wooden grandstand was destroyed by fire in April 1956. The playing field remained in use for many years until the North Greenwood Recreation and Aquatic Complex was built. On March 19, 2016, the site was recognized as a Florida Heritage Site, the first such honor in Clearwater.

Jack Russell Stadium

Jack Russell Stadium 1955 (City of Clearwater)

Jack Russell, a former Major League pitcher who had a 15-year career (1926-40) with six clubs, was a City Commissioner in Clearwater and former president of the Clearwater Chamber of Commerce. He was the leading proponent for a new ballpark for the city and Phillies. Final city approval came on May 20, 1954, and a $317,563 contract was awarded to the Clearwater Construction Company.

The opening game was March 10, 1955, with Robin Roberts facing the Detroit Tigers. A two-run double by third-baseman Willie Jones gave the Phillies a 4-2win. Over the years, additional seating increased the original 4,700 capacity to 7,000. A new clubhouse/office structure was added in right field, and an artificial turf infield was installed beyond the right field wall.

For many years after the Phillies left spring training, the field was reconfigured for the Bombers' softball season, moving home plate much closer to the stands. Prior to the next spring training, the city would again change the field back to baseball. When the Florida Stated League granted Clearwater a franchise on September 26, 1984, it meant the Bombers would have to relocate creating protests by the team and its fans.

The Clearwater Phillies played their first game against the Tampa Tarpons at home on April 12, 1985. The last spring training game was March 28, 2003, a 2-0 win for the New York Yankees before 7,224 fans. Pat Burrell got the last hit. Roberts threw out the ceremonial first ball 48 years after he threw the first pitch.

The very last game was August 23, 2003, a 6-2 Clearwater loss to the Sarasota Red Sox. Ryan Howard got the very last hit and made the last out. Roberts again tossed the ceremonial first ball.

Because of deteriorating concrete, the main grandstand was demolished on July 21, 2007, and replaced by bleachers. The Clearwater Department of Parks and Recreation manages the stadium, which is used by Clearwater High School, Saint

Petersburg Jr. College baseball teams, and youth amateur tournaments.

In 2018, the City unveiled Monument Park, a series of bronze plaques commemorating the stadium's history, Hall of Famers who played there, including the Phillies, and the 1980 World Champion Phillies.

Spectrum Field

Spectrum Field (Clearwater Threshers)

In 2004, a new ballpark in Clearwater opened four miles east of Jack Russell Stadium and adjacent to Carpenter Complex. It would serve as the Phillies spring training facility and home for the Clearwater Phillies, who changed their name to Threshers. The outfield dimensions and configuration are modeled after Citizens Bank Park, as is the 360-degree concourse open to the playing field. The park seats 7,000 fans. A grass berm beyond the outfield wall can accommodate as many as 2,000 fans.

The facility covers a total of 17.5 acres previously the site of a Home Depot store. The $31.5 million project was funded through a unique public-private partnership that included the State of Florida, Pinellas County, the City of Clearwater under Mayor Brian J. Aungst, and the Phillies.

On January 20, 2004, the Phillies and Bright House Networks announced the naming rights, Bright House Networks Field. Six years later, the name was shortened to Bright House Field. In 2017, the complex was renamed Spectrum Field after Bright House was purchased by Charter Communications.

The Phillies defeated the New York Yankees in the first game, 5-1, on March 4, 2004. Marlon Byrd got the first hit, and Jimmy Rollins the first home run.

Jersey Shore BlueClaws

The BlueClaws moved to Lakewood, NJ, from Fayetteville, NC where they had been known as the Generals. Their first season in Lakewood was 2001. Lakewood has led the South Atlantic League in either average or total attendance every year since and became the fastest team in South Atlantic League history to reach the two and three million fan attendance mark.

Originally known as the Lakewood Blue Claws, the team changed its name to the Jersey Shore Blue Claws in October of 2020.

Ballpark
First Energy Stadium opened in 2001 as GPU Energy Park (General Public Utilities Inc.). Merger next year with First Energy Corporation changed the name.

Managers
Gregg Legg (2001, 2014), Jeff Manto (2002), Buddy Biancalana (2003), PJ Forbes (2004-05), Dave Huppert (2006), Steve Roadcap (2007-08), Dusty Wathan (2009), Mark Parent (2010), Chris Truby (2011), Mickey Morandini (2012-13), Shawn Williams (2015-16), Marty Malloy (2017-18), Mike Micucci (2019).

Climbing the Ladder
(2001) C Carlos Ruiz; (2002) 1B Ryan Howard, RHP Gavin Floyd; (2003) LHP Cole Hamels; (2004) RHP Kyle Kendrick, (2005) RHP Carlos Carrasco, LHP JA Happ; (2007) C Tuffy Gosewisch, RHP Kyle Drabek; (2008) OF Domonic Brown, C Travis d'Arnaud, SS Freddy Galvis, LHP Jake Diekman, RHP Vance Worley; (2009) RHP Trevor May.

(2010) 1B Darin Ruf, OF Domingo Santana, IF Jonathan Villar; (2011) OF Aaron Altherr, 3B Maikel Franco, C Cameron Rupp, RHP Hector Neris; (2012) RHP Ken Giles; (2013) SS JP Crawford, OF Roman Quinn; (2014) C Willians Astudillo, C Deivy Grullon, C Andrew Knapp; (2015) 1B Rhys Hoskins, 2B Scott Kingery, LHP Josh Taylor; (2016) RHP Seranthony Dominguez, RHP Jacob Waguespack; (2017) OF Adam Haseley, LHP Ranger Suarez, LHP JoJo Romero, RHP Sixto

Sanchez; (2018) RHP Ramon Rosso, RHP Connor Brogdon, RHP Spencer Howard; (2019) 3B Alec Bohm.

Team Notes

Championship Teams: (2006, 84-55 record) Defeated the Augusta GreenJackets in the Championship Series ... (2009, 78-58) Defeated the Greenville Drive in the Championship Series... (2010, 84-55) Defeated the Greenville Drive in the Championship Series.

Championship Finals: (2016, 74-65) Lost to the Rome Braves in the Championship Series ... (2018, 87-51) Lost to the Lexington Legends in the Championship Series.

(2017) LHP Nick Fanti was involved in two no hitters: May 6 vs. Colombia (RHP Trevor Bettencourt got final out) and July 17, complete game gem vs. Charleston.

(2017) 1B Darick Hall named the league MVP, the first BlueClaw to win the award. He had a stellar season with 28 doubles, 27 home runs, 96 RBIs, and a .272 batting average in 426 ABs.

(2018) RHP Spencer Howard tossed a no-hitter in the playoff series against the Kannapolis Intimidators.

First Energy Park -Lakewood – Michael Dill

Lakewood Game Action – photo by Michael Dill

Photo by Michael Dill

Photo by Michael Dill

Short Season

Short-season baseball is where many professional baseball players begin their careers. These leagues are generally considered a step above rookie level leagues, and often include recently drafted college players or younger players who have graduated from the rookie level. Over their history, the Phillies have had nine player development contracts at the short-season level.

Schedule (60-65 games) runs from mid-June until Labor Day. The leagues generally start around the time that the amateur player draft has occurred, and extended spring training has been completed for players not assigned to full-season squads out of spring training. They are primarily teaching levels of play that acclimate new players to professional baseball life.

Chronology of Short-Season Affiliations
Huron, SD – Northern League – 1965-1968
Batavia, NY – New York Penn League – 1967
Eugene, OR – Northwest League – 1967-1968
Walla Walla, WA – Northwest League – 1969-1971
Auburn, NY – New York Penn League – 1972-1977
Bend, OR – Northwest League – 1979-1987
Utica, NY – New York Penn League – 1986-1987
Batavia, NY – New York Penn League – 1988-2006
Williamsport, PA – New York Penn League – 2007 – 2020

Huron Phillies

Pro baseball was initially played in the South Dakota city by the Huron Packers in the Dakota and South Dakota League from 1920-21. For four seasons (1965-68) Huron was the short-season hub of the Phillies playing in the Northwest League.

Following his playing career, Dallas Green joined the player development department headed by Paul Owens, director of minor leagues and scouting. Owens recommended that Green begin by managing in the minor leagues. The idea was for Green to experience life in baseball's lowest level. It was a road Owens had traveled. Green started at Huron in 1968 and moved to Pulaski, VA, the following season.

Ballpark
Memorial Ball Park. The stadium was built in 1950 and was financed by donations. It is a unique ballpark with its amphitheater style seating in the grandstand. The stadium continues in use today; amateur teams utilize the field.

Managers
Joe Lonnett (1965-67), Dallas Green (1968).

Climbing the Ladder
Among the players who began the climb to the majors in Huron: (1965) RHP Billy Champion, C Mike Compton. (1966) C Larry Cox, OF Larry Hisle, LHP Ken Reynolds, 3B John Vukovich, 38. (1967) SS Toby Harrah, 1B Andre Thornton. (1968) 1B Greg Luzinski, C-INF Manny Trillo.

Team Notes

Hisle hit .433 in 60 at-bats but fell short of qualifying for the batting title (66 at-bats to qualify) ... Luzinski led the league with 13 homers and 45 RBI in his 57-game season, both club records.

Batavia Trojans/Clippers/Muckdogs

For 20 seasons, Batavia, NY, was home to a Phillies minor league team, 1967 and then a 19-year stint (1988-2006). The 1967 club was known as the Trojans. The Phillies returned in 1988 as the Clippers before changing names to the Muckdogs ten years later.

Professional baseball in Batavia began in 1897 when a club played in the New York State League. Batavia celebrated its 80th anniversary during the 2019 season as the only founding member of the New York-Penn League still in existence.

Ballpark

The new Dwyer Stadium opened in 1996 replacing the original park that was built in 1937. However, the playing field remained as first constructed. It was initially called State Street Park and was a WPA project. During World War II, the name was changed to MacArthur Stadium after General Douglas MacArthur in an act of patriotism. Before the 1973 season, the stadium found its final name, Dwyer Stadium, after Edward D. Dwyer, a long-time team president who was instrumental in keeping the team in Batavia.

Managers

Max Lanier (1967), Don McCormack (1988-89), Ramon Aviles (1990-92), Dave Cash (1990), Tony Scott (1990), Al Leboeuf (1993-95), Floyd Rayford (1996), Greg Legg (1997, 1999) Frank Klebe (1998, 2000-01), Ronnie Ortegon (2002), Luis Melendez (2003-04), Manny Amador (2005), Steve Roadcap (2006).

Climbing the Ladder

Over the course of twenty seasons, a lot of players wore a Batavia uniform. For many, Batavia was the first rung on the ladder to the big leagues. Those who had major league careers of five-plus seasons include (1988) RHP Andy Ashby; (1989) RHP Steve Parris; (1990) RHP Mike Williams; (1991) RHP Mike Grace, RHP Tyler Green; (1992) C Gary Bennett; (1993) INF Kevin Sefcik, RHP Wayne Gomes; (1994) OF Wendell Magee; (1995) 2B Marlon Anderson; (1997) C Johnny Estrada, LHP Randy Wolf; (1998) OF Jason Michaels, INF Nick Punto, RHP Geoff Geary, RHP Carlos Silva; (1999) OF Marlon Byrd, RHP Ryan Madson; (2000) 2B Chase Utley; (2001) 1B Ryan Howard, RHP Alfredo Simon; (2002) OF Michael Bourn, RHP Jean Machi, RHP Brad Ziegler; (2004) LHP J.A. Happ, RHP Kyle Kendrick; (2005) C Tuffy Gosewisch, C Lou Marson, RHP Carlos Carrasco, LHP Jesse Outman, LHP Mike Zagurski; (2006) OF Quintin Berry, RHP Drew Carpenter.

Team Notes

Utley hit .307 in his pro debut, 2 homers, 22 RBI in 40 games ... Howard, .272, 6 HR, 35 RBI, 48 games in pro debut.

Eugene Emeralds

The Phillies and the Eugene (OR) Emeralds had a 10-year relationship in minor league baseball (1964-73). From 1966 to 1968, they were a short-season club (80-game schedule) in the Northwest League. In a co-op arrangement, the Phillies and Cardinals each provided players in 1966.

Ballpark

Bethel Park was one of the last wooden parks used in minor league baseball. It was built in 1949 and became home to the Eugene Larks in 1950, and then the Eugene Emeralds, 1955-68. Bethel Park was known as a pitcher's park and often had high wind conditions ... in night games there were "black spots" in the outfield which tormented fielders.

After the 1968 season, it was torn down for what was initially expected to be part of a highway ... later, Lark City Park was built on part of the old outfield.

Managers

Hal Luby (1966), Bobby Malkmus (1967), Nolan Campbell (1968).

Climbing the Ladder

C Mike Compton, C Buck Martinez, and 1B Andre Thornton wore Eugene uniforms during the short-season years.

Walla Walla Bears/Phillies

Another Phillies short-season team in the Pacific Northwest was the Walla Walla club, which had a player development contract with the Phillies from 1969-71 in the Northwest League.

223

During the first season, the team was known as the Bears. For the other two seasons, Phillies. The initial professional franchise in the community was 1891, a team known as the Walla Walla Walla Walla's. Tough to fit that name on a jersey.

Ballpark
Borleske Stadium was originally built in 1926. It is the current home of a collegiate summer league baseball team and hosts games for Whitman College Baseball and the Walla Walla High School football team.

Managers
Howie Bedell (1969), Gary Powell (1970-71).

Climbing the Ladder
Five players who began their pro careers in Walla Walla climbed to the majors. (1969) RHP Ron Diorio. (1970) 1B-OF Bob Beall, RHP Dave Downs. (1971) 1B-OF Dane Iorg, RHP Roy Thomas.

Team Notes
Downs is the last Phillies pitcher to toss a shutout in his major league debut, 1972 vs. Braves. He made three more starts for the Phils that season … 21-year-old 1B/OF Dane Iorg led the league in hitting with a .367 batting average in his first year as a pro. Of the Walla Walla Phillies group, he had the longest big-league career, 10 years. He made his MLB debut with the 1977 Phillies. Dane was traded in a package the following season to the Cardinals for Bake McBride …

Roy Thomas was the Phillies first round draft pick in 1971. Four years later, he was included in a trade with the White Sox for Jim Kaat. Thomas pitched eight years in the majors.

Auburn Phillies

For six seasons, the Phillies had a team in Auburn, NY (1972-77). Auburn first joined the New York-Penn League in 1958. The only year the city went without a pro team was in 1981. In 1978, the team name was changed to the Sunsets, as players were supplied by the Phillies and Indians under a co-op arrangement. The current Doubledays' franchise has been with the Nationals since 2011.

Ballpark
Falcon Park was originally built in 1927. It was demolished in 1994 and a new park was built on the same site. The Phillies played in the original one.

Managers
Nolan Campbell (1972), Harry Lloyd (1973), Larry Rojas (1974), June Raines (1975), Mike Compton (1976), Ruben Amaro Sr. (1977).

Climbing the Ladder
The following started their climb to the majors in Auburn and played a minimum of five seasons in the show: (1972) C Bill Nahorodny. (1973) OF Rick Bosetti, LHP Randy Lerch, RHP Dan Boitano. (1974) OF Lonnie Smith, RHP Jim Wright. (1975) Dickie Noles. (1976) INF Luis Aguayo, Ozzie Virgil. (1977) OF George Vukovich, 1B Greg Walker, RHP Jerry Reed. (1978) OF Alejandro Sanchez.

Team Notes
The 1973 club (46-23) won the league championship.
Rick Bosetti led the league in stolen bases with 27 and hit
.333 in 282 AB's.

Bend Phillies
For nine years, the Phillies fielded a team in Bend, OR, in the
Northwest League (1979-87). Originally the team was called
the Central Oregon Phillies. When the franchise was sold in
1981, the name changed to the Bend Phillies.

Ballpark
Municipal Stadium was built in 1964. Eighteen years later it
was renamed Vince Genna Stadium in honor of the city's
director of parks and recreation and long-time coach
of American Legion baseball teams.

Managers
Tom Harmon (1979), P.J. Carey (1980-81; 1985), Roly de
Armas (1982), Jay Ward (1983), Ramon Aviles (1984),
Ed Pebley (1986), Mel Roberts (1987).

Climbing the Ladder
(1979) SS Julio Franco, OF Alejandro Sanchez. (1980) 2B Juan
Samuel, OF Jeff Stone, C Jerry Willard. (1981) 3B Rick Schu.
(1982) OF Chris James, RHP Mike Maddux. (1984) RHP
Marvin Freeman, RHP Todd Frohwirth. (1985) INF-OF Rick
Parker, RHP Jason Grimsley. (1986) RHP Andy Ashby, INF
Steve Scarsone.

Team Notes

Franco (23 seasons) and Samuel (16) had the longest big-league careers … Schu and Maddux played and coached in the majors… Willard was one of five players traded for Von Hayes … Frohwirth scouted for the Orioles after his big league career ended … Parker was part of a major deal with the Giants that brought Terry Mulholland, Charlie Hayes, and Dennis Cook to Philly … Grimsley was dealt for Curt Schilling … Ashby became a 2-time All-Star … Scarsone has been in player development with the Diamondbacks and A's since his playing career ended.

In 1979 Bend defeated the Walla Walla Padres in the Championship Series.

Utica Blue Sox

Utica, NY, is another community in which the Phillies had a minor league working agreement twice, 1943-50 and 1986-87. The second time around, the Utica Blue Sox franchise was in the short-season New York-Penn League, bottom rung of a six-team Phillies minor league system.

Ballpark

Donovan Stadium. Currently, the ballpark is home to the amateur Utica Blue Sox who play in the Perfect Game Collegiate Baseball League and is also used for American Legion baseball.

Manager

Tony Taylor.

Climbing the Ladder

In each of the two seasons, Utica's roster was the youngest in the Phillies system, 19.2 years of age and 19.5. Those who went on to major league careers of five or more seasons were (1986) RHP Jason Grimsley, LHP Chuck McElroy, RHP Scott Service; (1987) RHP Andy Ashby, SS Kim Batiste.

Bend, OR, Genna Stadium: Charles O'Reilly

Huron, SD, Memorial Ballpark: Charles O'Reilly

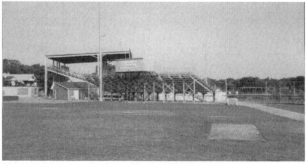

Utica, NY, Donovan Stadium: Charles O'Reilly

229

Walla Walla, WA, Borleske Stadium: Charles O'Reilly

Auburn, NY, Falcon Park I: ballparkreviews.com

Batavia, NY, Dwyer Field: ballparkreviews.com

Williamsport Crosscutters

Professional baseball in Williamsport dates to 1923 when the Williamsport Grays were formed. Two of the most important boosters and financial backers of the team were J. Walton Bowman and Thomas Gray. The Grays were in operation till 1962. Various franchises had affiliations in Williamsport from 1964-91.

The Crosscutters franchise was born in 1994. It was originally the Geneva Cubs, a team that played in Geneva, NY. They moved to Williamsport. The name Crosscutters reflects the logging heritage of Williamsport, once known as the "Lumber Capital of the World."

The Phillies began their short-season affiliation with the Crosscutters in 2007 as an ongoing member of the New York-Penn League and played there for 13 seasons with the final season of play being 2019. On November 30th of 2020, it was announced that the Crosscutters agreed to become a charter member of the newly formed MLB Draft League as part of the reconstruction of minor league baseball.

Ballpark
Bowman Field was completed in 1926 to host the Williamsport Grays. During its first three years, the ballpark was known as Memorial Field because of its location inside of the surrounding park. By 1929, the Grays club officials deemed it appropriate to name the field "Bowman Field" in honor of Gray's club president, J. Walton Bowman, who had been the main force in raising the money to build the facility.

In the summer of 2017, the first MLB Little League Classic game took place during the Little League World Series. The stadium was upgraded to conform to MLB's standards. A new playing surface with better drainage was installed along with padded fencing and new seating.

Bowman Field is the second-oldest ballpark in the minor leagues. It is presently the baseball home to both the Crosscutters and the Pennsylvania College of Technology Wildcats.

Managers
Gregg Legg (2007), Dusty Wathan (2008), Chris Truby (2009-10), Mickey Morandini (2011), Andy Tracy (2012), Nelson Prada (2013), Shawn Williams (2014), Pat Borders (2015-19).

Climbing the Ladder
(2007) OF Domonic Brown, SS Freddy Galvis, OF Michael Taylor, LHP Jake Diekman, RHP Joe Savery; (2008) C Travis d'Arnaud, RHP Kyle Drabek, RHP Vance Worley; (2009) 1B Darin Ruf, IF Jonathan Villar; (2010) OF Aaron Altherr, 2B Cesar Hernandez, C Cameron Rupp, OF Domingo Santana, LHP Jesse Biddle; (2011) 3B Maikel Franco, LHP Adam Morgan, RHP Hector Neris; (2012) OF Roman Quinn; (2013) OF Dylan Cozens, C Andrew Knapp; (2014) C Deivy Grullon, 1B Rhys Hoskins; (2015) RHP Jacob Waguespack; (2016) RHP Seranthony Dominguez, LHP Cole Irvin, LHP Ranger Suarez, LHP JoJo Romero; (2017) OF Adam Haseley, RHP Spencer Howard, RHP Connor Brogdon, RHP Ramon Rosso; (2018) 3B Alec Bohm.

Bowman Field – Williamsport, PA (Williamsport Crosscutters)

Rookie Level

Rookie league baseball is perhaps the most enthusiastic level of professional baseball that one can watch. It's the initial point of participation for most players. There's little fanfare. In fact, there are very few fans who actually attend. It's raw baseball where teaching is primary, and mistakes are aplenty.

"Baseball on the backfields" provides the foundation of each player's future development. It's a vital element of the equation. While some players may skip over, or spend less time in game action at this beginning step in their careers, there are none that aren't included in the initial teaching and guidance given by the instructors at this level.

Chronology of Rookie League Affiliations
Pulaski, VA – Appalachian League – 1969-1975
Helena, MT – Pioneer League – 1978-1983
Carpenter Complex, FL – Gulf Coast League – 1984; 1999 to present
Martinsville, VA – Appalachian League – 1988-1998
Dominican Republic – Dominican Summer League – 1993 to present
Venezuela – Venezuelan Summer League – 1998-2015

Pulaski Counts/Phillies
There are few communities in which the Phillies had minor league teams three separate times. One being Pulaski, VA. The Pulaski Counts of the Class D Appalachian League were one of 15 Phillies minor league teams in 1949. They returned from 1952-55. Fourteen years later (1969) the Phillies were back for a third stint, this time for seven seasons ... the Pulaski Phillies in the same league but a rookie level classification.

Pulaski has a history in pro baseball dating back to 1942 when the Counts franchise played in the Virginia League. The city has been a long-standing member of the Appalachian League, dating back to 1946, and remains a league member today.

Ballpark
Calfee Park was built in 1935 as part of the WPA (Works Project Administration) project. It's listed on the National Register of Historic Places. The park was named for Ernest W. Calfee who was the mayor when it was built. It's gone through multiple renovations and continues to serve as a home for Appalachian League pro baseball.

Managers
Dallas Green (1969), Brandy Davis (1970), Harry Lloyd (1971-72), Bob Wren (1973-75). Wren was Mike Schmidt's collegiate coach at Ohio University.

Climbing the Ladder
Pulaski was the starting point for many young players. Some advanced to brief major league careers. Those with five-plus big-league seasons include: (1969) OF Mike Anderson, LHP Mike Wallace. (1970) C Jim Essian. (1971) OF Jerry Martin. (1972) RHP Larry Christenson. (1973) SS Todd Cruz, RHP Jim Wright. (1974) RHP Mark Clear, LHP Kevin Saucier.

Team Notes
(1969) Pulaski won the Northern Division title (38-28) and defeated the Johnson City Yankees in the Championship Series.

(1969) Mike Anderson, 18, first-round selection that summer out of Timmonsville, SC, High School, had an impressive debut: .364 (4th in AL), 60 RBI (2nd), 84 hits (2nd), 18 doubles (2nd), 6 triples (tied for 1st) and 10 home runs (tied for 3rd) ... (1974) C Don McCormack wound up managing for eight seasons in the Phillies minor league system ... (1975) LHP Carlos Arroyo is a long-time minor league pitching coach in the Phils minors.

Helena Phillies
Working your way from rookie ball to the bright lights of Major League Baseball is a long journey. For six years, young Phillies' hopefuls got their feet wet in pro ball with the Helena Phillies in the rookie level Pioneer League (1978-83). The journey from Helena, MT, to Philadelphia is just over 2,200 miles. Some made it, others saw their dreams vanish.

When the Phillies established a working agreement with Helena in 1978, it ended a 64-year absence of pro ball in that community. Helena's previous team (Senators) played in the Treasure State League but disbanded in 1914.

Ballpark
Legion Field was built in 1932 to serve American Legion baseball. The cost was a whopping $1,500. Capacity, 2,100. It was renamed twice, once Memorial Park Field and then in the 1970s, Kindrick Legion Field in honor of Ace Kindrick, long-time supporter of Legion baseball in the community.

The ballpark has a classic covered grandstand and a scenic view of Mt. Helena. And, it is still in use by local American Legion teams and a collegiate summer league.

Managers
Larry Rojas (1978), Roly de Armas (1978-81), Ronald Smith (1982), P.J. Carey (1983).

Climbing the Ladder
Those that had big-league careers of five or more seasons: (1978) OF George Bell, OF Carmelo Castillo, OF Bob Dernier, OF Alejandro Sanchez, SS Ryne Sandberg. (1979) RHP Jay Baller, RHP Roy Smith. (1980) C Darren Daulton. (1981) RHP Charles Hudson. (1982) RHP Lance McCullers. (1983) 1B Ricky Jordan.

Team Notes
Bell (AL 1987) and Sandberg (NL 1984) wound up winning MVPs; Sandberg became a Hall of Famer … Daulton, 3-time All-Star. Dutch, Hudson, and Jordan played on Phillies' pennant winners and McCullers' son pitches for the Houston Astros.

Martinsville Phillies
Twice the Phillies had a minor league team in Martinsville, VA. First was a two-year (1940-41) stint in Class D. The second time was an 11-year run (1988-98) in the Appalachian League.

Ballpark
Hooker Field. In the 1930's Jim English built English Field, which has hosted professional and amateur baseball in Martinsville for several decades. With financial help from

Hooker Furniture, whose main plant is just down the hill from the ballpark, English Field was renovated in 1988 and was renamed Hooker Field. The Martinsville Mustangs, a collegiate summer team have used the ballpark since 2005.

Managers
Roly de Armas (1988-92), Ramon Henderson (1993-96), Kelly Heath (1997), Greg Legg (1998).

Climbing the Ladder
Martinsville was the first step for many youngsters. Some never reached the majors, some for a short time, and others had longer careers in the show: (1988) RHP Toby Borland; (1989) RHP Bob Wells; (1990) C Gary Bennett, C Mike Lieberthal; (1991) RHP Ricky Bottalico; (1993) C Bobby Estalella, 3B Scott Rolen; (1994) RHP Jason Boyd; (1995) RHP David Coggin; (1996) SS Jimmy Rollins, RHP Carlos Silva; (1997) RHP Derrick Turnbow; (1998) Ryan Madson.

Pulaski, VA, Calfee Park: Charles O'Reilly

Helena, MT, Kindrick Field: Charles O'Reilly

Martinsville, VA, Hooker Field: Charles O'Reily

Photo by Steve Potter

242

Gulf Coast League Phillies

The current version of the Gulf Coast League was formed in 1966. There had been three prior iterations dating back to 1907-08, 1926, and 1950-53. The present structure of the league began in 1964 with four clubs and was known as the Sarasota Rookie League; it expanded in 1965 to six teams and was renamed the Florida Rookie League. It became the Gulf Coast League a year later.

The Phillies' participation in the GCL started with the 1984 season. They didn't field a team again till 1999, a 15-year gap. During that time, the Phillies maintained their rookie level development in different forms often placing extra teams at higher levels.

The Phillies expanded to two GCL teams (East & West) in 2018.

Ballpark

Carpenter Complex is the home of the GCL Phillies. The games are usually played on either the Richie Ashburn or Robin Roberts Field. There is no admission fee with the contests generally being held at noon each day. While there are bleachers, the shade provided by the clubhouse is considered premium seating, and players, scouts and fans alike often congregate next to the walls to avoid the hot Florida sun. It's often where many of Steve Potter's best baseball conversations take place!

Oh, while spectators are sparse. Seagulls are plentiful.

Managers
Roly de Armas (1984, 2001, 2004, 2007-19), Ramon Aviles (1999-00), Ruben Amaro Sr. (2002-03), Jim Morrison (2005-06), Nelson Prada (2018), Milver Reyes (2019).

Climbing the Ladder
Many players have reached the majors: (2000) 3B Travis Chapman; (2001) RHP Alfredo Simon; (2002) RHP Scott Mathieson (2003), RHP Kyle Kendrick; (2004) RHP Carlos Carrasco; (2006) OF Domonic Brown, LHP Antonio Bastardo, RHP Kyle Drabek – traded for Roy Halladay; (2007) C Travis d'Arnaud, LHP Jake Diekman; (2008) RHP Trevor May; (2009) OF Aaron Altherr, SS Freddy Galvis, 2B Cesar Hernandez, 1B Darin Ruf, OF Domingo Santana, IF Jonathan Villar; (2010) 3B Maikel Franco, LHP Jesse Biddle; (2011) RHP Ken Giles;(2012) C Willians Astudillo, OF Dylan Cozens; (2013) SS JP Crawford, C Deivy Grullon; (2014) RHP Seranthony Dominguez, LHP Josh Taylor; (2015) LHP Ranger Suarez, RHP Jacob Waguespack; (2016) RHP Sixto Sanchez; (2017) OF Adam Haseley, RHP Ramon Rosso (2018) 3B Alec Bohm.

Team Notes
League Champions: (2002) 39-21 record; defeated Dodgers in Championship Series, 2-1 … (2008); 33-25 record; defeated Nationals in Championship Series, 2-1 … (2010) 32-24 record; defeated Rays in Championship Series, 2-1.

The Phillies team with the highest winning percentage was the 2016 club, a 43-15 record; lost to the Cardinals in the Championship Series, 2-1.

The 2019 GCL West team qualified for the playoffs with a record of 33-15 but the playoffs were cancelled due to Hurricane concerns.

Waiting for game action – Mark Wylie

GCL Action – Mark Wylie

GCL Action -Roberts Field – Mark Wylie

GCL Action – Ashburn Field – Danie Berlingis

Photos courtesy of Phillies

Dominican Summer League Phillies
The Phillies made a significantly larger investment in player development in the DSL when they built their own Academy. It opened in 2017. Prior to that, they had leased four different sites over the initial years of fielding their own team

from 1996 to 2016. Building their own academy was a big step forward.

In 2016 the Phillies began fielding two teams in the DSL (Phillies1 and Phillies2). A year later with the official Academy opening, the teams were re-named Phillies Red and Phillies White.

Ballpark
Boca Chica is the home to the Phillies 85,000-square feet training facility which sits on 45 acres. Opened as a shared facility with the Minnesota Twins. Each of the team academies has three full-sized fields, bullpen mounds, agility field, covered batting cages, dormitory space, dining hall, weight room, training room, video coaching room, and three classrooms for English language and Spanish instruction in multiple high school-level topics. The teams share a kitchen facility, an auditorium, and a maintenance building.

Life in the Academy is more than just baseball as Jesse Sanchez of MLB wrote: "All DSL players -- most teams have around 80 -- live at their academies and their day usually starts at 5:30 a.m. with breakfast. There's just enough time to lift weights and get early batting and fielding practice before the first pitch at 10:30 a.m. each day. After the games, the prospects eat lunch and go to class. They usually have dinner between 7 p.m. and 8 p.m., followed by a little free time before bed. There are no DSL games Sunday."

Graduation ceremonies at the Phillies' academy are held as the result of the educational classes. Players receive high school diplomas, something that they may have not achieved if not in the academy.

Managers

Wilfredo Tejada (1995-1996), Alberto Fana (1997), Alejandrito Taveras (1998-1999), Sammy Mejia (2000-2005), Domingo Brito (2006-2010), Manny Amador (2011-2016), Waner Santana (2017-2019), Orlando Munoz (2018-2019)

Climbing the Ladder

There have been multiple Phillies players who've advanced to the big leagues; however, records are only available beginning with the 2006 season: (2006) LHP Yohan Flande; (2008) IF Jonathan Villar; (2010) Hector Neris; (2012) Seranthony Dominguez; (2014) Edgar Garcia; (2017) Ramon Rosso.

DSL History

The league was founded in 1985 and joined by the Venezuela Summer League (VSL) three years later. The earliest Phillies involvement was 1993 when they shared a team with the Giants and Astros. They shared a team with the Cardinals (1994-95). The following season, the Phillies fielded their own team. The Phillies team was listed as a "working agreement" until 2009 when it became shown as an affiliate.

When the VSL disbanded after the 2015 season the DSL became the sole Latin America-based, professional summer league.

Currently, every major league team has an affiliate in the league. Fourteen clubs, including the Phillies, have two teams.

A total of 45 teams play in the six-division league.

Venezuelan Summer League Phillies

The Phillies continue to maintain a training academy in Venezuela. They had affiliated teams, either shared with other MLB organizations or singularly sponsored, in the VSL from 1998 to 2015. The league disbanded after the 2015 season.

Managers

Kennedy Infante (also Camp Coordinator) - 1998 to 2000, Rafael Delima (also Camp Coordinator) - 2000 to 2012, Trino Aguilar (also Camp Coordinator) - 2012 to 2015 - coordinator for off-season VZ Paralela League 2016 to 2017, Orlando Munoz (Camp Coordinator) 2016 to Present Day.

Climbing the Ladder

Players who reached the major leagues that played for the Phillies in the VSL include: (2005) RHP Sergio Escolana;(2007-08) 2B Cesar Hernandez; (2009-11) UTL Willians Astudillo (2011) RHP Severino Gonzalez; (2012) RHP Ricardo Pinto; (2012-14) LHP Ranger Suarez; (2013-2014) RHP Edubray Ramos

Carpenter Complex

Photo courtesy of the Phillies

Carpenter Complex

When the Phillies big league club began spring training in Clearwater in 1947, their minor league camps were scattered all over the south. 21-year-old pitcher Dallas Green got to experience that first-hand in 1956, his first year of spring training. In the space of seven weeks, he went from Clearwater to Plant City, FL (triple-A camp) to Bennettsville, SC (Class A camp).

Paul Owens, a scout based in Bakersfield, CA, was assigned to the Phillies Class A spring training camp in Leesburg, FL, in 1964-65 as coordinator of instruction. The rest of their minor leaguers (Class AA and AAA) were in Dade City, FL. Not an ideal arrangement.

Owens was promoted to Farm Director in Philadelphia early in the 1965 season. He decided the organization needed a training facility in Clearwater for all the minor league players. His vision included a large clubhouse in the middle, surrounded by four fields. Once he convinced owner Bob Carpenter, the Phillies and City of Clearwater negotiated an agreement to have a new facility built, sandwiched between Old Coachman Road and Route 19.

The new facility was financed by a no-interest $250,000 loan from the Phillies to the City of Clearwater which repaid the amount over years. While the Phillies were the primary tenant, the City also used the fields for various baseball programs.

During the dedication ceremonies on March 5, 1967, Clearwater Mayor Joe Turner announced the new facility would be known as Carpenter Field, in honor of the family that owned the Phillies since 1943. The new facility officially opened nine days later. At some point, the facilities' name was changed from Carpenter Field to Carpenter Complex.

With a training facility now in place, Owens started a fall Instructional League program. Training facilities at Jack Russell Stadium were limited. So, the big club, for many years, held daily spring training workouts at the Complex until the Grapefruit League games began. With the availability of four fields, multiple pitching mounds, and batting cages more work could get done in less time.

In 1984, the Phillies placed a team in the Gulf Coast League, a short-season league for young prospects not advanced enough for higher classifications. Games are played at the Complex.

The City of Clearwater, during the 1997-98 offseason, renovated the clubhouse. The original clubhouse structure was gutted and reconstructed to include a second floor. Improvements included a larger athletic training room, more offices, a large meeting room, and new lockers. Roof-top observation areas for the team's staff were now part of the second level. The project was completed in time for spring training in 2010.

When Bright House Networks Field was opened in 2004 adjacent to the Complex, the Phillies had one of the finest major league/minor league facilities in Florida.

Photo by Lee McDaniel

Paul Owens Training Facility

The clubhouse was named the Paul Owens Training Facility at Carpenter Complex in 2004 in honor of Owens' legacy of service to the Phillies organization. His bronze bust, located on the west side of the clubhouse, was unveiled on February 22, 2012.

After World War II, Owens, known to everyone as the "Pope", returned to his roots in Salamanca, NY. He was headed for a teaching career when the Olean team invited him to try out in 1951. He viewed it as a summer job while on teaching break.

He paid 75 cents to get into the park. The GM said it wasn't a try out, rather he needed him on the field. Owens got a couple of hits the first game and signed a contract for $175.00 per month. Four years later, the Phillies purchased the Olean club, which had been an independent team and Owens was a player-manager for the 1956-57 seasons.

Gene Martin, then the Phillies director of the minor leagues, moved Owens to Bakersfield, CA, to manage the California League team in 1958-59. Martin then convinced Owens to become a scout, giving him the entire southwest territory. Considering himself a "field person", he reluctantly changed his career path.

When Owens became farm director, his first item was to prepare for the first summer draft in June. After that he began to reorganizing scouting and player development, making numerous personnel changes.

Seven years later he was promoted to General Manager where he became the architect of the 1980 World Champions. Twice he put himself in the dugout. Shortly after becoming GM, he replaced his friend, Frank Lucchesi, as manager. Paul's mission: to find out who could play and who couldn't. If they couldn't play, they would be gone. At age 59, he returned to the dugout in the middle of the 1983 season and led the Phillies to the National League pennant.

The Pope did it all, player, minor league manager, scout, farm director, general manager, and manager in the majors. It can be said that he single-handedly turned the Phillies franchise around and may well be the best "baseball" man in club history.

Photo by Miles Kennedy

David P. Montgomery Baseball Performance Center

The crowning gem at the Complex came in January 2013 with the completion of a $4 million, 20,700 square-foot structure, the first indoor climate-controlled training center at a major league spring training site. Used year-round for training, workouts, and rehabilitation, the facility houses a weight room (7,200 square feet) and six indoor batting cages and pitching mounds (13,500 square feet).

Montgomery, a Philadelphia native, passionate Phillies fan, and University of Penn graduate, joined the organization in 1971 as a member of the sales department. A few years later, he became director of sales and marketing. When Bill Giles put together a group that purchased the Phillies from the Carpenter family, Montgomery was elevated to Executive President. He was the number one man under Giles, the team president. When Giles left in 1997 to become chairman, Montgomery was named president and CEO.

Under his presidency, the Phillies won five straight division titles, two National League pennants, and the 2008 World Championship. He oversaw the design and construction of Citizens Bank Park in Philadelphia and a new ballpark in Clearwater. Both opened in 2004, the first time a baseball franchise opened two facilities in the same year. Part of Montgomery's annual summer schedule included visiting every Phillies minor league team and spending time with the respective staffs.

Montgomery took a leave of absence in January 2014 to undergo treatment for jaw cancer. He became chairman when he returned the following year with Giles becoming chairman emeritus.

In spring training of 2018, the organization surprised Montgomery by naming the indoor training facility the David P. Montgomery Baseball Performance Center. The ceremony took place in front of the large red building with all the organization's players, baseball operations personnel, spring training front office staff, and Clearwater staff. He passed on May 8, 2019, at age 72.

Photo by Mark Wylie

1979 Spring Training – courtesy of Larry Shenk

Photo by Mark Wylie

Photo by Miles Kennedy

Leesburg Spring Training

Leesburg Spring Training - Photo courtesy of Larry Shenk

Leesburg Spring Training

Phillies minor league players were split among different locations for spring training for many years. In 1964, through 1966, their Class A players trained in Leesburg, FL, while AA and AAA clubs were 36 miles south in Dade City, FL.

Ruly Carpenter, 24-year-old son of Phillies owner Bob Carpenter, spent spring training in Leesburg in 1965, working under Clay Dennis, then the farm director. The idea was for Ruly to experience and learn all aspects of player development.

"I was the camp administrator which meant overseeing the business aspects," he recalled. "Players got a small stipend as meal money every week. Everybody stayed in this old hotel, the Magnolia. It was an ancient wooden building. Floors creaked when you walked on them. Two elderly ladies owned and operated the place. They got paid on a weekly basis.

"With five Class A teams, we had something like 130-140 players, housed two per room. Five managers, trainers, Dennis, myself, and Paul Owens comprised the rest of the camp."

Owens was a Phillies scout in Southern California, living in Bakersfield. For the second straight year, he spent spring training in Leesburg as the camp coordinator, organizing the daily workouts. "It was the first time I met him," explained Ruly. "I quickly learned how much he knew about the game. His judgment of players was unmatched."

Everybody walked to Pat Thomas Stadium for the workouts. When spring training was over, the Leesburg A's of the Florida State League played there. 18-year-old Rollie Fingers made his pro debut that season going 8-15 as a starting pitcher. He wound up in the Baseball Hall of Fame.

Practices took place at the Stadium and a couple of nearby fields. Players wore baggy, flannel, hand-me-down uniforms with no names on the jerseys. "It took a while to learn names," recalled Ruly. "Owens put me to work pitching batting practice, shagging, hitting ground balls to infielders."

After the workouts, the staff would crowd into a tiny hotel meeting room to review the day and discuss the players. "From those discussions and what I observed, our minor league system was void of talent. I played in the Ivy League and none could have played at that level." A handful eventually made it to the majors, each with a very brief career.

As happens at the end of every spring training, players get released. "Most unpleasant part of my job, telling kids they were being sent home. We had one guy, I think from Panama, who became incensed, so much so that he threatened to burn down the hotel. It would have taken only one match. I called the police, they came and handcuffed him. An officer and I drove him to the Leesburg airport and made sure he got on the plane."

Ruly also recalled a humorous story after spring training had ended.

"I was driving the Phillies' station wagon back to Philadelphia and got pulled over in Georgia. The sheriff said, 'Where you've been son?' I told him I was in spring training with Phillies' minor leaguers in Florida and heading back home. He said, 'A good friend of mine's son is a pitcher with the Phillies.' He mentioned a name which I've since forgotten but I remember saying, 'Oh, yea. He's a good prospect and should play in the majors soon.' The cop said, 'Good to know. I'm going to let you off this time but slow down.' The truth is that we had just released the kid," he said laughing.

Owens moved into the front office at Connie Mack Stadium after the season started to oversee scouting and player development, replacing Dennis. First order of business was to prepare for baseball's first summer draft.

"He and I had some on and off conversations about the bad spring accommodations for the minor leaguers," Ruly said. "He felt the players needed to train in one location. We and a couple other people went to Dodgertown in Vero Beach that summer to see the facility. All Dodgers players, majors and minors, trained there. At some point, Paul convinced Dad to build a complex in Clearwater. Paul's vision became a reality in 1967."

Centralized, consistent instruction and player evaluation were now possible. The entire instructional staff got to see every player in the system. An old era ended but a new era began in Clearwater.

Florida Instructional League

The concept of the Florida Instructional League (FIL) was founded in 1958 and initially consisted of four teams (Athletics, Braves, Cardinals & Yankees). The basic concept has not changed ... it's an introduction camp held at the team spring training complex for newer players to educate them on what is to come in the following year's spring camp while also emphasizing coaching focus on honing players' skills. Additionally, it's a place where relatively inexperienced players come after their pro season, and where experienced players might come to rehabilitate from injury or perhaps learn a new position.

In 1963, the FIL formalized a fifty-two-game schedule, and in 1967, the Phillies participated for the first time in the league, which at that point consisted of twelve teams.

Andy Seminick and Larry Shepard co-managed the '67 FIL Phillies. However, the organization was not void of a Fall League program prior to 1967. They sent a team to the Southern California Winter League in 1957, and were an annual participant in the Peninsula Winter League held in San Francisco, California from 1959 (Frank Lucchesi was the initial skipper) to 1968 when it disbanded. They cut over exclusively to the Florida FIL beginning in 1969 ... players participated in the Phillies 1969 FIL, twenty reached the majors including Bob Boone, Larry Bowa, Greg Luzinski, and John Vukovich, all core players during the winning era of 1975-84 (872-693).

The current day FIL emphasis is on individual training, and is not as formalized into game action against other clubs. The length of the endeavor has also drastically shortened over the years ... the 2020 Phillies fall instructs camp held at Carpenter Complex in Clearwater, Florida was four weeks long during the month of October. With the 2020 regular minor league season lost to the Covid pandemic, Fall Instructs were even more important, as they were, for many, the only opportunity to get on the field as an organization. Participating in the 2020 FIL camp were all four of the Phillies recent June draft selections along with the twelve undrafted free agent pitchers they signed after the draft concluded. A total of sixty-five players attended the camp.

Base-running instructions at 2020 Fall Camp - Photo by Mark Wylie

Catching Coordinator Ernie Whitt teaching at 2020 FIL Camp - Photo by Mark Wylie

2020 Fall Instructs game action vs Blue Jays - Photo by Mark Wylie

2020 4th round draft choice Baron Radcliffe gets instruction at camp – Mark Wylie

Dickie Noles and the late Roy Halladay at previous Florida Instructs Camp – Mark Wylie photo

Development Staff

Player development as an administrator, manager, coach, scout, or support person often involves long hours and dedicated effort. Those who do the jobs well have a shared passion for the game of baseball that becomes a bond in their joint endeavors. There's little if any public acknowledgment of their work, yet they are vital to the game's ongoing success.

The Phillies have had quite a few employees who have dedicated a huge part of their life to player development. They love teaching the game, watching their students do well, and are like proud parents when a ballplayer they've tutored reaches the major leagues. In this chapter, we will highlight some who have had, or continue to have long tenures within the Phillies Minor League system. They represent the true owners of the backfields of baseball.

Longest Service as a Phillies Minor League Manager

Roly de Armas – 31 years and counting
Bill Dancy – 19 years
Bob Wellman – 16 years
Greg Legg – 16 years
Frank Lucchesi – 14 years
Andy Seminick – 11 years
Dusty Wathan – 10 years
Ramon Aviles – 10 years
Dick Carter – 9 years
Lee Elia – 9 years

Jim Gott, Dan Plesac and Carlos Arroyo – Miles Kennedy

Carlos Arroyo

He never lived his dream of being a major league ballplayer, but Carlos Arroyo helped many kids fulfill their dreams. After a short career as a minor league pitcher, followed by 37 years as a coach in the player development department, Carlos stepped down after the 2020 season. Chances are, every Phillies minor league pitcher, who reached the majors, was schooled by Carlos.

In 2012, he received the John Vukovich Award, which is given annually to an instructor who embodies the characteristics of the award's namesake: loyalty, dedication, competitiveness, knowledge, honesty, and a terrific work ethic. It is an award that truly describes Carlos.

Playing Career

It was a transaction that got little attention when the Phillies signed a 15-year-old left-handed pitcher out of Vega Alta, Puerto Rico, in 1974. At age 16, he was the opening day starter for the Pulaski Phillies in rookie ball (1975). He moved up to single-A Spartanburg (1976) and to high-A Peninsula (1977), where he made the league's All-Star team and was named the loop's best left-handed pitcher. Carlos went 11-4 in 20 starts for AA Reading as a 19-year-old (1978).
He spent the next three seasons at AAA Oklahoma City. Carlos moved to the bullpen at that level and led the 89ers in saves (13) in 46 appearances in 1980.

He retired as a player, after pitching in Mexico (on loan from the Phillies) in 1982, as a result of an elbow injury.

Coaching Career

Began with extended spring training, which was held in Sarasota at the time (1983), followed by an assignment to Bend as a member of the short-season staff. In 1984, he was the pitching coach at Peninsula, one of only three minor league pitching coaches in the Phillies organization then.

Between 1985 and 2001, he served as pitching coach in Spartanburg, Clearwater, Reading, Batavia, Reading, Martinsville, Piedmont, Reading. That's a lot of bus rides.

In 2001, he was also asked to be a mentor for RHP Vincente Padilla with the big-league club for two seasons, but continued to help various other Latin born pitchers acclimate to life in the majors. From there, he assisted in the coordination of a pitching program for the Phillies' Dominican Republic and Venezuelan academies, while also performing as pitching coach for the GCL Phillies. Carlos became the minor league rehab pitching coach in 2010, and held that position thru the 2012 season.

Except for 2014, when he took on extra duties as the minor league pitching coordinator, Carlos served as the minor league roving pitching coach from 2013 to 2020.

Carlos said that before he left Puerto Rico as a 16-year-old, he was given a few words of wisdom from his mother ... "Be kind and treat others with respect" ... values he continued to take to heart and that are certainly applicable to us all, especially as we encounter and address struggles ... definitely words to live by.

Photo by Joe Stinger

Lee McDaniel

Lee McDaniel is the Director of Minor League Operations and is based at Carpenter Complex in Clearwater, Florida. Lee has been with the Phillies organization for twenty-four years and was awarded the Richie Ashburn/David Montgomery Award in 2018, considered the highest honor for any Phillies employee. He began his professional journey in Martinsville, VA ...

"I started in March 1990 as an operations intern for the Martinsville (VA) Phillies in the Appalachian League. Later that winter, I accepted my first full-time job with the Asheville Tourists (Astros at the time) in the South Atlantic League. I was there for two years as an assistant general manager for ballpark operations and sales in 1991-92. Just a few years before I arrived in Asheville, the movie Bull Durham was popular. At the very end of that movie, when Crash Davis was signed late in his career to play in Asheville, there is a scene where he drives up to the front entrance of the ballpark at old McCormack Field. My office was next to the front gate in that scene, so I always love to watch the end of that movie to remember what it all looked like. LOL."

After the '92 season in Asheville, I finished up a Masters in Sports Administration at Ohio University in March of 1993, at which time I received an offer from the Phillies to become the General Manager back in Martinsville. The owner of the franchise at that time was Tim Cahill, who also owned the franchise rights to the Danville Braves in the Appy League. Tim offered the position upon my graduation that March, and I was there until the end of the 1995 season.

In September 1995, Phillies Director of Florida Operations, John Timberlake, offered me a position in Clearwater at Jack Russell Stadium as an assistant general manager for Spring Training and the Florida State League club. Carlos Arroyo, Ramon Henderson, Jerry Martin, and other coaches from the Appy League club all put in a good word for me with Timberlake, so I'm forever indebted to them. I worked at Jack Russell from 1995-99, then moved over to the Carpenter Complex in Player Development Administration in January of 2000. I've been at the complex since that time."

Memories

"I was born in Martinsville, VA, and raised in a nearby community called Horsepasture, VA. So, to get my start there with the Phillies was literally a dream come true. The Phillies played Appy League home games at Hooker Field in Martinsville. I played many games there as a youth growing up in the area. The ballpark naming rights during the Phillies era was with Hooker Furniture, which was a prominent furniture factory in town, located just behind the RF fence. When I was growing up in that area in the late 60s, 70s, and 80s, the field was called Red English Field and was a historic site for semi-pro baseball dating back to the WWII days. My father played there in the 40s and later in the 50s post-WWII.

The ballpark was also home to Martinsville High School, where a young man by the name of Lou Whitaker played in the mid-70s as an amateur. Other local players that had professional baseball careers include catcher J.C. Martin (Cubs/Mets), catcher Randy Hundley (Cubs), Randy's father Cecil Hundley who was a long-time scout for the Cubs, Monty Montgomery (Royals), Roy Clark (long time director of scouting for the Braves), and many other players that were drafted/signed over the decades. Ton of history in Martinsville!"

Challenges of Minor League Life

"Working in professional baseball is definitely a lifestyle. Probably the biggest challenge is the number of hours we all put in on a year-round basis, especially during the season between the beginning of Spring Training to the end of the instructional league in late October. Our families have to sacrifice a great deal to work around our seven days per week schedule. I'm very blessed and fortunate that I don't travel a great deal, and can go home at the end of each day. Our coordinators, coaches, athletic trainers, strength coaches, and support staff are all away from their families for a very long time each year, and truly sacrifice their family time to work in professional baseball."

Favorite minor league town, ballpark, restaurant, or hotel ...

"Ahhh – too many to name! My all-time favorite has to be Reading. They have a classic throw-back ballpark that has wonderfully captured its baseball history through artifacts, photos, and memorabilia throughout the park -- and they are second to none in entertainment. The front office staff are like family to all of us – as is the case with all of our affiliates. A close second would be Asheville. My first year there in 1991 was the last year of the old historic McCormack Field, which at that time was the 2nd oldest ballpark in the country, I believe. Great restaurants there. Beautiful mountains nearby. Very scenic place."

Photo courtesy of Phillies

Johnny Almaraz

Johnny took over as the Phillies Director of Amateur Scouting in 2014 and held that position until after the 2019 draft. He started in pro baseball in 1988, when he was drafted by the Cincinnati Reds as a pitcher. After he retired as an active player, he went on to be the Director of Player Development with the Reds, and later the Director of Latin America Operations and Director of International Scouting and Operations with the Atlanta Braves. He's widely considered "one of the most prolific talent evaluators in baseball". Here are some of his thoughts on life in the minor leagues, scouting, and player development.

A Challenging Life

"For many minor league players providing for themselves is very challenging in many shapes and forms. The requirements of everyday living come into focus ... often, it's the first time they've been on their own. In a multi-cultural world ... getting things to eat and getting around ... driving or even getting a car is difficult, especially if there are language barriers. A lot of it is also monetary ... funds are short so it makes it even harder."

Player Development Approach

"Everything works off the leadership ... the perspective of the approach. For example, when I was with Atlanta, Bobby Cox had a huge influence ... he was very big on making sure fundamentals were stressed and that trickled down to all levels. When changes occur in leadership personnel, the fundamentals of baseball are still core ... philosophy and technique may differ but there's always an inherited consistency in the game of building baseball knowledge."

Player Evaluation Keys

"Things like seeing a player swing the bat with authority, the Oldtimers used to say, to hear the whistle of the bat is key ...

strength is important. Good players come in all shapes and sizes .... scout for tools and ability ... that's the focus."

Players who make it to the show
"When a player makes it, you are proud ... it's almost like a parental relationship ... you want them to do well for themselves ... when they do the feeling is like being a proud dad."

Player Struggles
"Failing is a big part of succeeding ... over time that's changed a bit ... many only want to experience success. Failing is often more mental than physical ... that's a key to building ... positive reinforcement helps and is part of coaching but when a player learns to come back from failure, that in itself is a great learning experience."

Changes in development over the years
'Everything always evolves ... we are more impatient today with players ... probably a direct relationship to the exposure and coverage guys now have via social media, internet, prospect rankings, etc. ... those things are irrelevant to developing a player but there is more pressure to move guys up before they are ready ... expectations become higher."

Analytics
"They've been around a long time ... stats like OPS and guys like Bill James date pretty far back ... the applications have certainly changed in regards to the tools now available ... they solidify what scouts see ... for example a good curve ball is now supported by the reported spin rate ... we always knew it was a good curve when we saw it but now the data supports that. You still have to evaluate the game ... you still

have to watch in order to do that ... data and analytics are supports and validations."

Photo courtesy of Phillies

Manny Amador

Manny Amador began his Phillies career as a player. He began to play in 1993 as a member of the Martinsville Phillies as a seventeen-year-old shortstop. Manny played a total of six minor league seasons, reaching the Triple A level of play in 1997. He appeared in 467 minor league games and posted a .267 career batting average in 1,546 AB's.

Following the 1998 season, he turned his attention to coaching and player development. He became the hitting instructor for Phillies Dominican Summer League team in 1999 and held that position till 2001. During the 2001 season, he went to Reading to finish the season as the AA level hitting coach after John Kruk's departure there. Manny served as hitting coach for the Clearwater Phillies for the 2002 thru 2004 seasons and as Manager of Batavia in 2005.

In 2006, Amador took over managing the Phillies Dominican Academy operations. In addition to his administrative duties, he continued to work in player development as well. From 2011 to 2016, he also served as the DSL Phillies field manager.

When the Phillies opened their own Academy building in 2017, Manny was officially named as the Dominican Coordinator, his current position. He gets great joy in his job, saying that "seeing players reach their dreams is the best feeling I could ever feel." He notes that professional baseball is challenging, especially spending extensive time away from family. As an instructor, he says "When players are having tough times or struggling, I always try to build positive thinking and give them support ... of course we also work our butt off every day. I try to make everyone have a strong and positive mind."

"When a player reaches the big leagues ... first, I'm extremely happy for them. And second I'm super happy with myself and my team because I know that we just helped another guy to make his dream come true ... just to see how their life changes is amazing ... a priceless feeling!"

"Baseball has changed my perspective and life. I came from a very poor family, the Phillies became all that I had ... first as a player and after as a coach, this is the only organization that I have been with. I would like for it to really be the only one ever ... everything that my family and I have is because of the Phillies."

Manny has spent twenty-seven years in the Phillies' organization. His dedication and efforts are just as priceless as the feeling that he gets when a player reaches his goal. It's all part of it.

Roly de Armas greets Marcus Lee Sang - Mark Wylie

Roly de Armas

No manager or coach in the Phillies minor league organization can equal the experience or longevity of current GCL Phillies East manager Roly de Armas. He's on the top of the list with 31 years through 2019. De Armas also managed three seasons other than the Phillies.

He's been managing the Gulf Coast League Phillies continuously since 2001. His team won championships in

2008 and 2010. And, he's a yearly fixture as a manager or instructor on the Fall Instructional League staff.

Signed by the Phillies as an amateur free agent, Roly played in the organization for five seasons (1973-77). The only positions he didn't play were shortstop and outfield. While coaching with the 1993 Clearwater Phillies, de Armas saw his last action as a player, including two appearances on the mound. He appeared in 314 minor league games and compiled a .258 average. He hit one home run. It came in his first pro season (1973) with the Auburn Phillies.

Coaching/Managing, Phillies
1978 - Pitching Coach - Peninsula
1979-1981 - Manager - Helena, MT- Pioneer League
1982 - Manager - Bend, OR- Northwest League
1983 - Manager - Spartanburg, SC - South Atlantic League
1984 - Manager - GCL Phillies - Gulf Coast League
1985-1986 -Manager - Spartanburg, SC - South Atlantic League
1987 - Manager - Clearwater, FL - Florida State League
1988-1992 - Manager - Martinsville, VA - Appalachian League
1993 - Coach - Clearwater, FL - Florida State League
2001 – Manager - GCL Phillies - Gulf Coast League
2002-2003 - Manager - Clearwater, FL - Florida State League
2004 - Manager - GCL Phillies - Gulf Coast League
2005-2006 - Phillies Minor League Catching Coordinator
2007 - 2019 - Manager - GCL Phillies - Gulf Coast League

Elsewhere
1994-1996 - Chicago White Sox - MLB Bullpen Coach
1997 - Chicago White Sox - GCL Manager

1998 - Arizona Diamondbacks - Manager - South Bend, IN - Midwest League
1999 - Arizona Diamondbacks - Manager - AZL
2000 - Toronto Blue Jays - MLB Bullpen Coach

In 2008, he also served as a bullpen coach to finish the season with the World Champion Phillies. His GCL team was league champions, and he was a coach for Team USA in the Olympics. Quite a year!

Roly has been a coach for Team USA 10 different times and has participated in that accord in the Pan Am and Olympic Games, as well as the World Baseball Confederation.

De Armas won the John Vukovich Award in 2009. Started in 2007, the award is presented annually to an instructor in the Phillies organization who embodies the characteristics of the award's namesake: loyalty, dedication, competitiveness, knowledge, honesty, and a terrific work ethic.

To date, 146 of his players have reached the major leagues, a figure that includes 17 players from other organizations. Some had a cup-of-coffee career, others a much longer time in the show.

Roly's Phillies Roster
Pitchers
Marty Bystrom, Bob Walk, Cliff Speck, Jerry Reed, Jay Baller, Roy Smith, Rocky Childress, Marty Decker, Tony Ghelfi, Johny Abrego, Charles Hudson, Jose Segura, Mie Maddux, Lance McCullers, Jeff Gray, Tom Newell, Julio Machado, Bob Scanlan, Scott Service, Brad Brink, Chuck Malone, Chuck McElroy, Brad Moore, Toby Borland, Donnie Elliott, Paul

Fletcher, Jeff Patterson, Bob Wells, Mike Farmer, Ricky
Bottalico, Tony Fiore, Larry Mitchell, Ron Blazier, Jose De
Jesus, Wayne Gomes, Alfredo Simon, Ezequiel Astacio,
Jean Machi, Elizardo Ramirez, Zach Segovia, Scott Mathieson,
Kyle Kendrick, Carlos Carrasco, Kyle Kendrick, Antonio
Bastardo, Drew Carpenter, Carlos Monasterios, Justin
DeFratus, Jake Diekman, Tyler Cloyd, Yohan Flande, Trevor
May, Matt Smith, Jaren Cosart, Jesse Biddle, Lisalverto
Bonilla, Ken Giles, Yacksel Rios, Jesen Therrien, Drew
Anderson, Mark Leiter Jr., Edubray Ramos, Josh Taylor,
Seranthony Dominguez, Brandon Leibrandt, Austin Davis,
Miguel Gonzalez, Ranger Suarez, Jacob Waguespack,
Mauricio Llovera, Sixto Sanchez, Ramon Rosso.

Catchers
Darren Daulton, Mike Lieberthal, Gary Bennett, Bobby
Estalella, Lou Marson, Jason Jaramillo, Travis d'Arnaud,
Willians Astudillo, Deivy Grullon, Jorge Alfaro.

Infielders
Ken Dowell, Greg Jelks, Ken Jackson, David Doster, Jon Zuber,
Brad Harmon, Adrian Cardenas, Lendy Castillo, Jonathan
Villar, Jon Singleton, Darin Ruf, Cesar Hernandez, Freddy
Galvis, Jason Donald, Maikel Franco, Zach Green, Tommy
Joseph, J.P. Crawford, Alec Bohm.

Outfielders
Jim Olander, Keith Hughes, Chris James, Johnny Paredes,
Wilfredo Tejada, Rick Parker, Chris Roberson, Greg Golson,
Domonic Brown, Anthony Gose, Domingo Santana, Aaron
Altherr, Carlos Tocci, Cam Perkins, Dylan Cozens, Adam
Haseley.

Photo courtesy of Phillies

Bill Dancy

Bill Dancy spent 26 seasons in the Phillies minor league player development system. Nineteen of those were as a manager, second longest tenure in franchise history (1979-95; 1998-99).

He also served as Phillies' infield coordinator (2000) and field coordinator (2001-04; 2007-08). And, he was the major league third base coach for the Phillies (2005-06).

Phillies Managerial Career
1979 – Spartanburg (SC) Phillies – Western Carolinas League
1980-82 – Hampton (VA) Peninsula Pilots – Carolina League.
1983-85 – Reading (PA) Phillies – Eastern League
1985-86 – Portland (OR) Beavers – Pacific Coast League
1987 – Old Orchard (ME) Maine Guides – International League
1989-91 – Scranton/Wilkes-Barre (PA) Red Barons – International League

1992-93 – Clearwater (FL) Phillies – Florida State League
1994-95 – Reading Phillies – Eastern League
1998-99 – Clearwater Phillies – Florida State League

His teams reached the postseason six times. Championships came in 1980 (Peninsula), 1993 (Clearwater), and 1995 (Reading). Dancy was named the Eastern League Manager of the Year in 1983.

His best team was the 1980 Pilots, 100-40. Five players from the club reached the majors, SS Julio Franco, OF Will Culmer, LHP Don Carman, RHP Roy Smith, and RHP Warren Brusstar.

In addition to working for the Phillies, the baseball lifer has served in various player development roles with the Atlanta Braves, Chicago Cubs, Kansas City Royals, and the Detroit Tigers.

As a minor league skipper for 23 total seasons, he amassed 1,670 wins.

Prior to turning to player development Dancy played in the Phillies system (1973-78) and appeared in 525 games over six seasons; shortstop, second and third bases. He reached Triple A in 1975 and spent the last four seasons of his career at the AA/AAA levels. He finished with a .271 batting average.

Overall, Dancy has been in pro baseball for 47 years.

Photo courtesy of Larry Shenk

Bob Wellman

Bob Wellman had an impressive minor league career as a
player but only limited time in the majors. His dedication to
the game was his impressive career as a minor league
manager. He spent 16 seasons with the Phillies (1961-1975),
managing at every level. Before joining the Phillies,
he had five years as a player-manager in the Cincinnati Reds
organization (1955-59). His minor league managerial career
ended with four years with the New York Mets (1977-80)
after which he scouted for the club, 1981 into the 1990s.

A large man (240 pounds in a 6-foot-4 frame), he was
affectionately known as "Bear."

For many young Phillies players, Wellman was their first
manager. A total of 79 of his players reached the major
leagues. Four were on the 1980 World Champion Phillies,

Larry Bowa, John Vukovich, Warren Brusstar, and Keith Moreland.

Phillies Managerial Career
1961 - Dothan, AL, Phillies, Alabama-Georgia League
1962-63 – Bakersfield, CA, Bears, California League
1964-65 – Eugene, OR, Emeralds, Northwest League
1966 – Spartanburg, SC, Phillies, Western Carolinas League
1967-68 – Portsmouth, VA, Tides, Carolina League
1969 – Reading, PA, Phillies, Eastern League
1970 – Eugene, OR, Emeralds, Pacific Coast League
1971-72 – Spartanburg Phillies, Western Carolinas League
1973 – Rocky Mount, NC, Phillies, Carolina League
1974-76 – Reading Phillies, Eastern League

His overall record for 3,356 minor league games, 1,771-1,578, a .529 percentage. Wellman's teams reached the playoffs six times, won three championships of which two were with the Phillies, the 1966 and 1972 Spartanburg Phillies. The 1966 club was his best, a 91-35 record, setting a league record by winning 25 consecutive games. Five future major leaguers were on the team, SS Larry Bowa, 2B Denny Doyle, 1B Ron Allen and RHPs Barry Lersch, and Lowell Palmer.

As an outfielder-first baseman, Wellman played minor league ball for 15 seasons. His career numbers: 1,535 games, 348 doubles, 219 home runs, 400 RBI and a .315 average. Four times he led his league in home runs. His major league career was a total of 15 games with the Philadelphia A's, four in 1948 and 11 in 1950. Of his seven hits, one was a home run off Boston's Mel Parnell at Shibe Park in 1950. Even though he never returned to the big leagues, he was featured on a baseball card in the inaugural Topps set in 1952.

He died in 1994 in Villa Hills, KY, at age 69.

Greg Legg – Photo by Cheryl Pursell

Greg Legg

When it comes to longevity with the Phillies organization, Greg Legg is right up there. For four decades, he's been a player (13 years), minor league manager (16), and coach in the minors (10). Only Roly de Armas (31 years) and Bill Dancy (19) have managed longer with the Phillies. Oddly, Legg, an infielder, played on seven teams managed by Dancy.

Managerial Career

1997 – Batavia (NY) Clippers - New York-Penn League
1998 – Martinsville (VA) Phillies – Appalachian League
1999 – Batavia Muckdogs – NYPL

2000 – Kannapolis (NC), Piedmont Boll Weevils – South Atlantic League
2001 – Lakewood (NJ) BlueClaws – South Atlantic League
2002-04 – Reading (PA) Phillies – Eastern League
2005-6 – Clearwater (FL) Threshers – Florida State League
2007 – Williamsport (PA) Crosscutters – NYPL
2014 – Lakewood BlueClaws – SAL
2015-16 – Clearwater Threshers – FSL
2017-18 – Reading Fightin Phils - EL

Coaching Career
1994-95 – Clearwater Phillies
1996 – Scranton/Wilkes-Barre (PA) – International League
2008-13 – Lakewood BlueClaws
2019 – Allentown (PA), Lehigh IronPigs – International League

Four players from the first team he managed (Batavia) reached the majors, LHP Randy Wolf, C Johnny Estrada, LHP Thomas Jacquez, and 1B-C Andy Dominique. Six of Legg's clubs reached the playoffs. He was the inaugural manager of the Lakewood BlueClaws and the Williamsport Crosscutters, and followed Mike Schmidt in Clearwater, becoming the Threshers' second manager.

In 2008, he returned to Lakewood as hitting coach, but also received an interim assignment with the big-league team as bullpen coach when Roly de Armas went to the Olympics as a coach with Team USA. He continued his role as hitting coach with Lakewood thereafter thru the 2013 season.

Greg was drafted by the Phillies in the 22nd round of the 1982 draft out of Southeastern Oklahoma State as an infielder. He played the NAIA World Series all four years. Eleven of his minor league seasons were in triple-A. He compiled a .275 average in 1,184 minor league games. Legg played with five Phillies Wall of Fame inductees during his minor league years, Juan Samuel, Darren Daulton, Mike Lieberthal, John Kruk, and Curt Schilling.

His major league career included 14 games with the Phillies in brief stints, 1986 and 1987. His major league debut came against the New York Mets at Shea Stadium on August 18, 1986, as a seventh-inning replacement at second base. Greg's first hit was a pinch-hit single, eighth-inning off Bob Walk at Pittsburgh's Three-Rivers Stadium, April 27, 1986. His career average in the majors is .409.

Photo courtesy of Phillies

Frank Lucchesi

Frank Lucchesi could best be described as a baseball lifer. Following graduation from Galileo High School in San Francisco (alumni include Tony Lazzeri and the DiMaggio brothers), the 5-foot-8, right-handed hitting outfielder signed with the Portland Beavers (AAA, Pacific Coast League) as a 19-year-old in 1945. He spent five decades in pro ball, most years as a manager. Perseverance is another ideal description.

Seventeen of the years were with the Phillies, 14 as a minor league manager and three as "Skipper Lucchesi" in the majors. His teams finished in the first division eight times, reached the playoffs six times, and were champions three times.

Right-handed pitcher Dallas Green was on the first team Lucchesi managed for the Phillies. He helped guide the careers of many other youngsters on the way up. Among them Art Mahaffey, Bobby Wine, Chris Short, Dick Allen,

Fergie Jenkins, Pat Corrales, Larry Bowa, and Rick Wise. He also managed two 1950 Whiz Kids who were trying to resurrect their careers in the minors, Robin Roberts and Curt Simmons.

As the Phillies manager, Lucchesi had the distinction of winning the last game at Connie Mack Stadium and the first game at Veterans Stadium.

Phillies Minor League Managerial Career
1956 – Salt Lake City (UT) Bees – Pioneer League
1957-58 – High Point-Thomasville (NC) Toms – Carolina League
1959-60 – Williamsport (PA) Grays – Eastern League
1961 – Chattanooga (TN) Lookouts – Southern Association
1962 – Williamsport Grays – Eastern League
1963-65 – Little Rock (AR) Arkansas Travelers – International League
1966 – San Diego (CA) Padres – Pacific Coast League
1967-68 – Reading (PA) Phillies – Eastern League
1969 – Eugene (OR) Emeralds – Pacific Coast League

Minors Elsewhere
1951 – Medford (OR) Rouges – Far West League (no affiliation)
1952 – Thomasville (NC) Tomcats – Georgia-Florida League (no affiliation)
1953-54 – Pine Bluff (AR) Judges – Cotton States League (St. Louis Browns)
1955 – Pocatello (ID) Bannocks – Pioneer League (no affiliation)
1973 – Oklahoma City (OK) 89ers – American Association (Cleveland)

1981 – Charleston (WV) Charlies – International League (Cleveland)
1988-89 – Nashville (TN) Sounds – American Association (Cincinnati)

Major League Managerial Career
1970-72 – Phillies – National League
1975-77 – Texas Rangers – American League
1987 – Chicago Cubs – National League (interim)

Lucchesi was 24 years old when he turned to managing, serving as a player-manager, 1951-57. He managed every level, Class D, C, B, A, AA, AAA. His overall record for 23 seasons in the minors, 1,605-1,436.

He and umpires didn't always see eye-to-eye. He was fined and suspended once for yanking the cap off an umpire's head and throwing it on the ground. He was known to pile dirt on home plate after ejections. Once in Little Rock, after getting tossed, he climbed a water tower beyond the outfield fence to continue managing. The same ump noticed him and motioned him to leave the tower. And, on "Frank Lucchesi Night" in Williamsport he got ejected in the third inning.

The Previous Structure Years

Minor League baseball was more disjointed, with multiple levels of classifications prior to 1963, when the classifications were adjusted to create the outline of the present structure. Prior to the restructure from the lowest level to the highest, leagues were classified as D, C, B, A with some designated as AA and a handful as AAA. Class D was a long way from the majors.

The Phillies had player development agreements with 72 different franchises between 1934-1962. Eight of those were designated as AAA level of play, three in AA and eight at the A level. The remaining fifty-three franchises played at the B thru D levels. The B thru D classifications are in inverse ranking with B being the higher level of play and B, C, and D being lower in subsequent order. In chronological order within each classification:

Montgomery Bombers-Class B-1938 -Montgomery, AL
In 1937, the Montgomery Bombers began play in the Southeastern League. The Phillies affiliated for one season and played at the Cramton Bowl (built 1922).

Manager: Bud Connolly

Team Notes: 19-year-old OF Harry "The Hat" Walker, property of the Phillies in 1938-39, only one on the roster to have a significant major league career. NL batting champion (.363) in 1947, playing for Cardinals and Phillies.

Pensacola Pilots -Class B – 1939-1940 -Pensacola, FL

Pensacola played in the Southeastern League, 1928-50. The Phillies had a two-year player development contract there and played at American Legion Park (built 1911).

Manager: Wally Dashiell

Team Notes: (1939) Defeated Jackson Senators in Championship Series. (1940) Lost Championship Series to Jackson.

****

Founded in 1896, the Interstate League's longest continuous operation was 1939-52. It was one of the few mid-level minor leagues to operate during WW II. The Phillies had working agreements in three different cities, Allentown, PA; Trenton, NJ and Wilmington, DE.

Allentown Wings -Class B – 1941 -Allentown, PA

Professional baseball in Allentown dates to 1884. In 1939, the team was known as the Dukes (Boston Braves), followed by the Fleetwings (Cardinals) and Wings (Phillies). Ballpark: Fairview Field.

Managers: Cy Morgan, Jimmy DeShong

Trenton Packers -Class B – 1942-1943-Trenton, NJ

The York (PA) White Roses (New York-Penn League) relocated to Trenton in mid-season 1936. Three years later, the Trenton Packers joined the league. For two seasons, the

Packers were affiliated with the Phillies. Games were played at Dunn Field.

Managers: Richard Lloyd, John Casey, Tony Rensa (1942); George Ferrell (1943).

Team Notes: (1943) OF Del Ennis, 18, made his pro debut, his only season in the minor leagues. He had a monster season: .346, 37 doubles,16 triples, 18 home runs; led the league in total bases (320). After spending the next two years in the military during WW II, he returned in 1946, went right to the majors, and became the first Phillies' rookie to be selected to the NL All-Star team.

Wilmington Blue Rocks -Class B-1944-1952 –Wilmington, DE

Wilmington sportsman, Bob Carpenter, had a vision of bringing minor league baseball to his hometown. A January 1939 meeting at Shibe Park with owner/manager Connie Mack of the Philadelphia A's helped bring the vision to life. The A's would provide the players if Carpenter built a ballpark. Wilmington was an affiliate of the Philadelphia Athletics from 1940-43 and the Phillies, 1944-52. Games were played in Wilmington Park. When the Interstate League disbanded after the 1952 season, the Blue Rocks franchise dissolved.

Managers: Fred Dorman, Ray Brubaker (1944), Cy Morgan, Ray Brubaker (1945), Jack Saltzgaver (1946-47), Jack Sanford (1948-49), Skeeter Newsome (1950), Danny Carnevale (1951) and Lee Riley (1952).

(1947) Defeated the Allentown Cardinals in the Championship Series. (1950) Defeated the Hagerstown Braves in the Championship Series. (1951) Defeated the Sunbury Giants in the Championship Series.

Team Notes: (1947) LHP Curt Simmons, 18, made his pro debut, 13-5, 2.69 ERA; joined the Phillies that September and never pitched in the minors again. (1948) RHP Robin Roberts made his debut, 9-1, 2.06 ERA for 11 starts and was promoted to the Phillies that June.

Portland Pilots -Class B – 1948-1949 – Portland, ME

Portland's franchise was created in 1946 and played in the New England League. The Phillies fielded a team there for two years, one of 15 minor league teams in their system. Games were played in Portland Stadium. The league folded after the 1949 season.

Managers: Del Bissonette (1948), Skeeter Newsome (1949).

Team Notes: (1949) Defeated the Springfield Cubs in the Championship Series.

Terre Haute Phillies -Class B – 1946-1954 – Terre Haute, IN

In 1946, the Philadelphia Phillies agreed to place a farm club in the Wabash Valley. The agreement almost did not happen until a meeting in Philadelphia with Terre Haute mayor Vern McMillan and Phillies owner Rob Carpenter. When the two men kicked up their feet on a table, they both noticed they had enormous holes in their souls. The two shared a good chuckle and sealed the deal to bring back minor league baseball in Terre Haute. - Stadium Journey

The Terre Haute Phillies were members of the Illinois–Indiana–Iowa League ... an organization that operated for the better part of 60 years. They played at Memorial Stadium which is the current home of the Indiana State football team. After the 1954 season, with attendance dwindling, the Phillies moved the franchise affiliation to Reidsville, North Carolina.

Managers: Ray Brubaker (1946-1947), Jack Sanford, Whitey Gluchoksi (1947), Dale Jones, Pat Colgan (1948), Lee Riley (1949), Danny Carnevale (1950), Skeeter Newsome (1951-1952), Hub Kittle (1953-54).

League Champions (1950 and 1952)

Team Notes: C Stan Lopata, 3B Willie Jones, RHP Bob Miller, members of the 1950 National League champions, each began their pro careers in Terre Haute.

Reidsville Phillies -Class B – 1955 – Reidsville, NC

The Reidsville Luckies played in the Bi-State League (1935–40) and returned in 1947 as part of the Tri-State League. They switched to the Carolina League in 1948 and remained there till the team was dissolved after the 1955 season. The team took its name from Lucky Strike cigarettes, which were produced by the American Tobacco Co. in Reidsville, NC. They played as the Phillies in 1955 during their one-year affiliation at Kiker Stadium.

Manager: Charlie Gassaway

Wilson Tobs -Class B – 1956 – Wilson, NC

The pro-level Wilson Tobs played periodically between 1908-1973. The Tobs nickname was a shortened form of the word "tobacconists". The team played in the Carolina League from 1956-68. They had a one-year affiliation with the Phillies and played at Fleming Stadium, built in 1938 by the WPA. It's still in use today as the home of the Wilson Tobs collegiate summer team.

Manager: Charlie Gassaway

Lewiston Broncs -Class B – 1957 – Lewistown, ID

The Lewiston Broncs played from 1952-74. Locally, the team was known as "Lewis-Clark" to include the adjacent city of Clarkston, WA. They played in the smallest town in America to have a professional baseball team, and were the only pro team to be operated without a business manager. During their entire existence, they were run by a board of directors centered on the stockholders.

The Phillies played one season at Bengal Field, which is now a high school football facility.

Manager: Hillis Lane

High Point-Thomasville Hi-Toms -Class B
1957- 1958 High Point, NC

The Thomasville Chair Makers were founded in 1937, and began play in the newly formed North Carolina State League. In 1948, the franchise was renamed the High Point-Thomasville Hi-Toms.

They joined the Carolina League in 1954. Three years later the Phillies began a two-year stint, playing at Finch Field.

Manager: Frank Lucchesi

Team Notes: (1958) LHP Chris Short, 20, was 13-13 in his second pro season; promoted to the Phillies that September.

Des Moines Demons -Class B – 1959-1961 Des Moines, IA
The Des Moines Demons played in the Illinois-Indiana-Iowa League (Three-I League), 1959-61. The team and league folded in January of 1962. The Phillies played all three seasons at Sec Taylor Stadium, which was built in 1947 and rebuilt/renamed in 1991 as Principal Park, the current home of the AAA Iowa Oaks.

Managers: Chuck Kress (1959, 1961), Andy Seminick (1960).

Wilmington, DE, 1948 Blue Rocks scorecard: Larry Shenk

Wilmington, DE, 1944 Blue Rocks scorecard: Bob Warrington

Terre Haute, IN, Memorial Stadium: Marc Viquez

Terre Haute, IN, Opening day: Marc Viquez

Terre Haute, IN, Phillies logo: stadiumjourney.com

Wilson, NC, Fleming Stadium: Charles O'Reilly

Thomasville, NC, Finch Stadium: Ballparkreviews.com

Des Moines, IA Sec Taylor Stadium: Charles O'Reilly

Des Moines, IA, Demons: iowacubs.com

The Class C Affiliations

Ottawa Senators -Class C – 1940 – Ottawa, ON

The Ogdensburg, NY, Colts were a Canadian-American League franchise from 1936-39, while the second iteration of the Ottawa Senators (first established in 1912) played in the league during the same time frame.

Ogdensburg partnered with Ottawa in 1940 to form a team, playing in both locations. The two-city franchise played as the Senators with half of their games in each city. (Winter Park in Ogdensburg and Landsdowne Park in Ottawa). The team was an affiliate of the Phillies.

Manager: Cy Morgan

Rome Colonels -Class C – 1942 – Rome, NY

The Rome Colonels were a Can-Am League franchise from 1937–42 and 1946–51. Pro Baseball in Rome dates as far back as 1898. The Rome Colonels were a one-year affiliate of the Phillies, who played at Colonels Park, which is today known as Franklyn's Field – a public park.

Managers: John Griffins, Phillip Clark

Greensboro Patriots -Class C – 1945 – Greensboro, NC

The Carolina League has existed since 1945. The league was officially announced on October 29, 1944, as a successor to the Bi-State League. Greensboro has been in the league, 1945-68. First year was with the Phillies, playing in the legendary War Memorial Stadium, which was used to film Bull Durham. It's still in play today as the home of NC AT&T collegiate baseball.

Managers: Wes Ferrell, Charles Burgess, Charles Eastman, John Allen

Schenectady Blue Jays -Class C- 1946-1950 -Schenectady, NY

The Schenectady Blue Jays origination was directly attributed to the Carpenter family. Coinciding with the family purchase of the Phillies after the 1943 season, the new ownership decided to expand their minor league footprint, and Schenectady was chosen as a new affiliate in the Can-Am League. The McNearney brothers (Pete and Jim), business partners in a beer company, were the franchise owners. They funded and built a new stadium (McNearney Stadium).

Managers: Bill Cronin (1946), Lee Riley (1947-48), Dick Carter (1949-50).

Team Notes: (1947) Riley, father of NBA legend Pat Riley, won his lone championship in his seven years as a Phillies minor league manager ... (1948) LHP Tommy Lasorda, in his first season following two years in the military service, struck out 25 Amsterdam Rugmakers in a 15-inning game (May 31) and drove in the winning run with a single. At the time the strikeout total was a professional record.

Salina Blue Jays -Class C – 1946-1952 – Salina, KS

The Salina Blue Jays joined the reorganized Western Association in 1946 as a Phillies minor league team. After seven seasons, the Phillies ended their affiliation, and pro baseball ended in Salina. The team played at Kenwood Field which opened in 1938. Forty years later, it was converted to a rodeo arena and renamed Tri-Rivers Stadium.

Managers: Edwin Walls (1946-47), Vance Dinges (1948), Joe Gantenbein (1949), John Davenport (1950), Pat Patterson (1951-52).

Team Notes: (1947) RHP Bubba Church, 22, made an impressive pro debut, 21-9, 2.93 ERA. Became one of the many home-grown players on the 1950 National League champion Phillies ... Following the 1943 season, the Phillies held a contest for a nickname. Winner was Blue Jays, which first appeared on the Phillies jersey in 1944. The Phillies had three minor league teams that season, Wilmington Blue Rocks, Elmira Blue Sox, Bedford Blue Wings. Four years later, two more teams were in the system, Schenectady Blue Jays, Salina Blue Jays.

Vandergrift Pioneers -Class C – 1947-1950 – Vandergrift, PA

The Pioneers were a team in Westmoreland County, Western Pennsylvania. They played in the Middle Atlantic League and were an affiliate of the Phillies throughout their existence. They played at Davis Field which was built in 1921 and currently is a youth football field. The franchise disbanded during the 1950 season due to financial difficulties.

Managers Pat Patterson (1947-48), Lew Krausse (1948), George Savino (1949), Don Hassenmayer (1950).

Team Notes: (1947) Defeated the Butler Yankees in the Championship Series. Club drew 87,000 fans even though the town's population was only 10,500. SS Alex Garbowski, 25, won the batting title (.396) in his second pro season. His only

315

big-league experience was as a pinch runner in two games for Detroit in 1952.

Salt Lake City Bees -Class C – 1951-1957 – Salt Lake City, UT
The franchise began in 1914. In 1939 the third version of the Bees came to fruition as a member of the Pioneer League. The Phillies became the first pro affiliate in the city and played there for seven seasons. They played at Derks Field which opened in 1915 as Community Park. The Stadium was razed in 1993 and a new ballpark was built on the site. It remains the home of the current Pacific Coast League Salt Lake City franchise.

Managers Hub Kittle (1951-52, 1955), Ed Murphy (1953), Charlie Gassaway (1953-54), Bobby Sturgeon, Sven Johnson (1956), Frank Lucchesi (1957).

Team Notes: (1953) Bees defeated Great Falls Electrics in the Championship Series … (1956) RHP Dallas Green was the ace of the staff, 17-12 … It was Lucchesi's first year of 14 in the Phillies minor league system, fourth longest in franchise history.

Grand Forks Chiefs -Class C – 1951-1952 – Grand Forks, ND
The franchise played in the Northern League from 1934-64 although not for the entire time. The Phillies had a two-year affiliation and played at Municipal Park, current site of a fire station. The franchise disbanded after the 1964 season.

Manager Ed Murphy.

Team Notes: Murphy played in 13 games with the 1942 Phillies and limited games with the Chiefs. None of the players in Grand Forks these two seasons ever reached the show.

Pittsfield Phillies -Class C – 1951 – Pittsfield, MA

The Pittsfield Electrics were a team from 1941-51. They played as the Pittsfield Phillies for the 1951 season, one of four Class C teams in their minor league system that year. When the Phillies arrived, expectations were of a new grandstand at the Wahconah Stadium but it wasn't ready, so the team played a portion of their games at a makeshift location, Dorothy Deming Field. Wahconah Stadium is still in use; Deming Field is a public park.

Manager Dick Carter

Granby Phillies -Class C – 1952-1953 – Granby, QC

In 1948 professional baseball formed in Quebec in the Provincial League. The new league included a new franchise in Granby. The Phillies had a two-year affiliation there and played at Granby Stadium. The team folded after the 1953 season and the Phillies moved to Trois-Rivière.

Manager Al Barillari

Trois-Rivière Phillies-Class C – 1954-1955 – Trois-Riviere, QC

The baseball team began as the Trois-Rivières Renards and played in the Quebec Provincial League and the Canadian-American League thru 1950. In 1951, the club moved to the Provincial League. The Phillies were there for the league's final two seasons.

Managers Snuffy Stirnweiss (1954), Al Barillari (1954-1955).

Bakersfield Bears -Class C -1956, 1958-1962– Bakersfield, CA

The longest-tenured Bakersfield pro baseball club was formed in 1941 as a charter member of the California League. The league was considered C level league through the 1962 season. The Phillies played there for six Class C seasons. Sam Lynn Ballpark, built by the WPA in 1941, was the venue. The Phillies continued their affiliation through the 1967 season with the league being classified as an A league.

Managers Art Lilly, Dick Wilson (1956), Paul Owens (1958-59), Lou Kahn (1960-61), Bob Wellman (1962).

Climbing the Ladder

(1958) SS Bobby Wine; (1959) INF-OF Danny Cater, C Pat Corrales, LHP Dennis Bennett; (1962) LHP Grant Jackson, RHP Bill Wilson, SS Mike Marshall.

Team Notes: Players who made their pro debuts in a Bears uniform: Wilson, Jackson, Wise ... (1958) Wine, 19, in second pro season, 13 doubles, 11 triples, 11 homers ...
(1959) Owens made his last appearance as a player, 1-3 in 1 game. In seven minor league seasons he compiled a .374 average; twice hitting .407 in the PONY League.

OF Johnny Callison was signed by the White Sox in 1957 after graduating from Bakersfield High School. Began his pro career that summer in his hometown. Phillies acquired him from the White Sox two years later in trade for 3B Gene Freese. One of the best Phillies trades ever.

Magic Valley Cowboys -Class C - 1961-1962 - Twin Falls, ID

The Magic Valley Cowboys formed in 1952 in the Pioneer League and played for a total of 17 seasons, 1952-71. The club affiliated with the Phillies for two seasons as a C level team and an additional season when the league was moved up to the A classification. They played at Jaycee Field, built in 1939 by the WPA. The site became Harmon Park, currently a public park with multiple sports fields.

Manager Jack Phillips

Climbing the Ladder

(1961) Dick Allen, OF Adolfo Phillips; (1962) 1B Hank Allen, LHP John Morris.

Team Notes: (1961) Dick Allen, in his second pro season, .317, 21 homers, 94 RBI; played second base
... 1B Costen Shockley, in his pro debut, finished second in the league with a .360 average; major league career was two brief seasons ... OF Bobby Sanders, league-leading 40 home runs and118 RBI, .325 average; career ended two years later with Class AA Williamsport ... (1962) 1B Hank Allen, 21 (Dick Allen's older brother, won the triple crown, .346 average, 37 home runs, 140 RBI. Played in the majors (Senators, Brewers, White Sox) for seven seasons. After his playing days concluded he had a long career as a scout.

Greensboro, NC, War Memorial Stadium: Charles O'Reilly

Trois-Rivieres, QC, CA, Stade Stadium: Charles O'Reilly

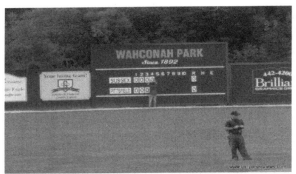

Pittsfield, MA, Wahconah Stadium: Ballparkreviews.com

Pioneer League: sportslogos.net

Bakersfield, CA, 1956 team photo: Michael Rinehart.

Bakersfield, CA, 1961 program: Michael Rinehart

Centreville Colts – Class D – 1938 – Centreville, MD

The Eastern Shore Baseball League was a Class D minor league that operated on the Delmarva Peninsula for parts of three different decades from the 1920s to the 1940s. It had teams from Maryland, Delaware, and Virginia but eventually disbanded due to lack of attendance revenue. The Phillies had a one-year player development contract with Centreville and played in Centreville Park, now a public park known as Quinn Anne Count Park. The baseball stadium no longer exists.

Manager: Joe O'Rourke

Mayodan Millers – Class D – 1939 – Mayodin, NC

The Bi-State League was formed in 1934 with teams in Virginia and North Carolina. The league played for nine seasons before disbanding. The Mayodan franchise existed from 1938-41. The Phillies affiliated for one season and played in Mayo Park which is now the site of the Mayodan United Methodist Church.

Managers: Harry Daughtry, Ramon Couto, Chink Outen

Johnstown Johnnies – Class D – 1939 – Johnstown, PA

The Pennsylvania State Association was a league that existed,1934-42. During the nine-year run of the league, there were eleven Pennsylvania cities that represented the league. The Phillies participated one season in Johnstown. They played at Point Stadium which opened in 1905 and remains in use today by high school and collegiate teams.

Manager: Dick Goldberg

Moultrie Packers – Class D – 1939-1940,1957 – Moultrie, GA

The town fielded teams within the Georgia-Florida League, 1935-63. (the league folded and reorganized four times over that time frame). They were affiliated with the Phillies for two full seasons and again for a few months in 1957. They played in Moultrie Stadium where the center field fence was 560 feet away! The ballpark was torn down in the 1960s and Colquitt County High School was built on the site.

Managers: Joe Holden (1939-1940), George Jacobs (1940), Benny Zientara (1957)

Team Notes: (1939) 19-year-old RHP Johnny Podgajny from Chester, PA was the youngest member of the team; 15-10, 31 games, 2.92 ERA for the first pro season. Made MLB debut with 1940 Phillies; 5-years in majors, Phils, Pirates, Indians (1940-46).

Portsmouth Cubs – Class D – 1939-1940 – Portsmouth, VA

The Piedmont League operated from 1920-55. Portsmouth had a franchise in the loop from 1935–55. The Phillies were linked to the club for two seasons. They played at both Sewanee Stadium (built in 1921) and Lawrence Stadium (built 1936). The Phillies returned to Portsmouth from 1966-68 when they affiliated with the Portsmouth Tides franchise.

Managers: Jim Keesey (1939), Ray Brubaker, Art McHenry, Bill Steinecke (1940)

Team Notes: (1940) 24-year-old LHP Max Wilson w 20-10 with a 3.02 ERA in 39 games (253 IP); also appeared in three big league games with the Phillies later in the season. He played a total of eight pro seasons - mostly in the minors, 99-61 in 202 games.

Wausau Timberjacks – Class D – 1940-1941 – Wausau, WI

The Wausau Lumberjacks (also known as the Timberjacks) existed on-and-off from 1905-57. The team played in the Northern League when the Phillies had a two-year affiliation. They played at Athletic Park which hosted minor league baseball for 36 seasons, 1936-90.

Manager: Wally Gilbert

Team Notes: (1940) 26-year-old 3B Chet Cishosz led the league in hitting with a .403 batting average (372 ABs); played just one more season in a seven-year minor league career.

Martinsville Manufacturers– Class D
1940-1941 –Martinsville, VA

The franchise existed from 1934-41 in the Bi-State League. They were affiliated with the Phillies for two seasons. Like most of the other clubs in the league, the team discontinued operations due to financial issues. The team played at Doug English Field which was built in the 1930s and hosted professional and amateur baseball for several decades. With financial help from Hooker Furniture, whose main plant was just down the hill from the ballpark, English Field was renovated and renamed Hooker Field where it hosted the Class A level Martinsville Phillies from 1988-98.

Managers: Harry Daughtry (1940), George Ferrell (1941)

Team Notes: (1940) The team defeated Bassett Furniture Makers in the Championship Series.

Dover Orioles – Class D – 1940, 1946-1948 - Dover, DE

The Dover Phillies were a team that played in the Eastern Shore League. The franchise began in 1923 and played four seasons. It disbanded and returned in 1937, the Phillies affiliated for the 1940 season. After World War II they continued as a Phillies affiliate for three more seasons after the Eastern Shore League reorganized. The team played at Oriole Park which was also known as Dover Baseball Park.

Managers: Cap Clark (1940), John Lehman (1946), Dick Carter (1947), Guy Glaser, Grover Wearshing (1948)

Team Notes: (1948) Posted one of the worst records in baseball history (26-100); finished 65 1/2 games behind first-place Salisbury, MD.

Bradford Blue Wings – Class D – 1944-1955 - Bradford, PA

Bradford had a long history of baseball dating back to the 1800s however the biggest impact of professional baseball came when the town became a 1939 charter member of the Pennsylvania-Ontario-New York League (PONYL). The franchise and Phillies entered a player development contract in 1944 that would last for 12 years. The team name was switched to the Phillies in 1950. They played at Community Park which was built in 1916. Today the former ballpark site is part of an oil refinery business campus.

Managers: Ray Brubaker, Ken Blackmon (1944), Lee Riley (1945-1946), George Savino (1947-1948), Danny Carnevale (1949), Barney Lutz (1950), Frank McCormick, John

Davenport (1951 and 1953), Dick Carter (1952), James Deery (1954) and Lew Krausse, Pat Colgan (1955).

Team Notes: (1949) The team won the league championship by defeating the Hamilton Cardinals in the Championship Series. 21-year-old RHP Roy Face, signed by the Phillies as an amateur player before the season, made his pro debut going 14-2 in 25 games (17 starts) amassing 141 IP and posting a 3.32 ERA. He would go on to pitch in 16 major league seasons with the Pirates, Tigers, and Expos from 1953-69. Face posted an incredible 18-1 record in 1959 in 57 relief appearances with the Pirates who won 78 games. Face accounted for 35% of their wins!

Concord Weavers – Class D – 1945 - Concord, NC

The North Carolina State League originally existed from 1913–17. The second version of the league was established in 1937 and operated thru 1953. The Concord Weavers played in the league from 1936-52. They were an affiliate of the Phillies for one season and played at Webb Park at Concord High School. The facility remains in use today.

Manager: John Lehman

Team Notes: 17-year-old LHP Tommy Lasorda made his professional debut; also played in the field. Finished with a 4.09 ERA in 27 games (121 IP). As a hitter, Lasorda played in 67 games, .274 in 208 at bats. He was the only player on the roster to reach the major leagues. Pitched in 26 MLB games from 1954-56 with the Brooklyn Dodgers & KC Athletics). We better know him as the Hall of Fame manager of the LA Dodgers for 21 seasons (1976-96).

Green Bay Blue Jays – Class D – 1946 - Green Bay, WI
The Green Bay Blue Jays played in the Wisconsin State League from 1940-53 and had a player development contract with the Phillies for one season. The team played at Joannes Stadium which was built in 1929 and continues to be used today.

Manager: Harry Griswold

Team Notes: The team won the league championship with a 76-36 regular season record; eight-team loop didn't have a playoff tournament.

Americus Phillies – Class D – 1946-1950 - Americus, GA
Multiple pro baseball clubs have called Americus home from 1902-2002 with the Phillies' five-year affiliation being the longest tenure. They played at Americus Ball Park which opened in 1938 and remains as one of the last wooden ballparks built by the WPA. Today it's owned and used by Americus-Sumter High School. The Phillies were the last major league team to have a player development contract in Americus.

Managers: Jack Sanford (1946-1947), Lew Krausse (1947), LeGrant Scott (1948), Ed Murphy (1948–50).

Team Notes: (1946) team went 87-37 in the regular season and lost in the Championship Series to the Moultrie Packers. That season, the pitching staff had two 20-game winners and another hurler who registered 17 wins ... RHP John Asmer set a league record for wins (24-6 with a 2.81 ERA in 35 games); RHPWilliam Murray, (21-6 in 33 games with a 3.22 ERA), and RHP Charles Dommer, (17-6 in 33 games with a 2.15 ERA). None played in the big leagues and all were out of baseball following the 1949 season.

Appleton Papermakers – Class D
1947-1949 - Appleton, WI
Appleton has been a steady home to Minor League Baseball since the 1940s. Originally named the Appleton Papermakers the still existing franchise is now known as the Wisconsin Timber Rattlers of the Midwest League.

The Phillies had a three-year player development contract with the franchise when they played in the Wisconsin State League. They played at Goodland Field which hosted baseball from 1940 till 1994. The site is now a sports complex owned by the Appleton School District.

Managers: Andrew Latchic (1947), Whitey Gluchoski (1947-1948), Frederick Clemence (1949)

Carbondale Pioneers – Class D
1947-1950 - Carbondale, PA
The team was formed in 1945 as a charter member of the newly organized North Atlantic League. The club's existence, as well as the North Atlantic League, was short ... the league folded after the 1950 season as did the Carbondale team.

The team played at Russell Park which was constructed by the WPA. Today it's part of a public park and is the site of the Carbondale Little League and area youth soccer fields.

Manager: Pat Colgan (1947-48), Barney Lutz (1949), Joe Glenn (1950)

Team Notes: The team won the league championship in both 1947 and 1948. They played in the 1946 Championship Series as well.

Ed Wade (former Phillies GM) grew up in Carbondale and had these memories: "Pat Colgan, the club's original manager, was the dad of Kevin Colgan, with whom I played at Russell Park while attending St. Rose High School. I began playing at the Little League field at Russell Park when I was four years old and moved on to 'the big' Russell Park for Teener League and American Legion games. Although Larry Shenk was the person who gave me my chance to work in Major League Baseball, it was the folks in Carbondale who spurred my ambitions, most of which centered around playing outfield for the New York Yankees, and stoked my love of the game."

Klamath Falls Gems – Class D
1948-1951 - Klamath Falls, OR

The Klamath Falls Gems were a charter member team in the Far West League. They were an affiliate of the Phillies for all four years that the league existed. The team played in Gems Stadium (now known as Kiger Stadium) which was built in 1947. It's still in use today by Oregon Tech University's baseball team.

Managers: Joe Gantenbein (1948), Hub Kittle (1949-50), William DeCarlo (1951).

Team Notes: (1951) team won the league championship defeating the Redding Browns in the Championship Series. 2B Stanley Roseboro led the league in hitting (.409 in 372 AB's) and triples (21).

Baton Rouge Red Sticks – Class D – 1948 - Baton Rouge, LA

The Evangeline League began in 1934. It ceased operations in 1942 during WW II but resumed activities in 1946 and lasted through 1957. The Baton Rouge Red Sticks played in the Evangeline League from 1946-55. They were a charter member. The Phillies had a one-year player development contract with the franchise and played at City Park.

Manager: Dick Carter

Seaford Eagles – Class D – 1949 - Seaford, DE

The Eagles played in the Eastern Shore League from 1946-49. The Phillies had a one-year player development contract with the franchise and played at Seaford Ball Park.

Manager: Paul Gaulin

Pulaski Counts – Class D – 1949, 1952-1955 - Pulaski, VA

The Phillies placed players on the roster but the primary player development agreement for Pulaski in1949 was with the Brooklyn Dodgers.   The Phillies would return to Pulaski three years later for a four-year stint and again in 1969 for a seven-year exclusive agreement in the Appalachian League. They played at Cafee Park.

Managers: George Pfister (1949), Al Gardella (1952-1953), George Triandos (1954), Ed Murphy (1955).

Lima Phillies – Class D – 1950-1951 - Lima, OH

The Lima franchise was born in 1939. In 1947, Lima joined the Ohio-Indiana League. For two seasons the team was known as the Lima Phillies, they played their games at Allen County Park on a makeshift field which was part of the fairgrounds. Today the site is part of a residential community. The Ohio-Indiana League faded away after the 1951 season, the victim of dwindling attendance.

Managers: Frank McCormick (1950), Barney Lutz (1951).

Elizabethtown Phillies – Class D – 1951 - Elizabethtown, TN

The Appalachian League of Professional Baseball began play in 1911. Elizabethton has been and continues to be a long-standing member of the league with multiple affiliations including the Phillies. For one season the Phillies fielded at team in E-Town, they played at Cherokee Park.

Managers: John Davenport, Donald Marshall.

Miami Eagles – Class D – 1952 - Miami, OK

The Kansas–Oklahoma–Missouri League (KOM) was established in 1946. It existed for seven seasons (1946-1952) as a Class D League. The Miami Eagles (also known as the Miami Owls and Miami Blues) played in the league during its entirety. The Phillies fielded a team in their final season. They played at the Miami Fairgrounds.

Manager: John Davenport

Team Notes: (1952) Eagles defeated the Ponca City Dodgers in the Championship Series. 18-year-old RHP Jim Owens went 22-7 in 36 games (245 IP) with a 1.76 ERA (led the league). Pitched in 12 big-league seasons with the Phillies, Reds, and Astros appearing in 286 games.

Mattoon Phillies – Class D – 1953-1956 - Mattoon, IL

Mattoon has an expansive history of professional baseball dating back to 1899. The last and longest-lasting pro franchise in Mattoon was formed in 1947 as a member of the Illinois State League which became the Mississippi-Ohio Valley League in 1949. Mattoon maintained a team in the league till it folded after the 1955 season. The Phillies had a four-year player development run with the franchise; played at Mattoon Baseball Park which was built in 1947 and demolished just ten years later in 1957.

Managers: James Deery (1953), Carl Bush, Don Osborne (1954), Burl Storie (1955), Benny Zientara (1956).

Team Notes: (1955) 20-year-old RHP Dallas Green made his debut, pitching in 11 games (55 IP) posting a 4-3 record and 3.44 ERA. (1956) 18-year-old RHP Art Mahaffey made his pro debut, 10 games, 4-4 record (75 IP) with a 5.28 ERA. He would pitch in 7 big league seasons (1960-66) with the Phillies and Cardinals.

Olean Oilers – Class D – 1956-1958 - Olean, NY

The New York–Penn League (NYPL) was founded in 1939 with the name Pennsylvania–Ontario–New York League (PONY). The Phillies had a long-standing affiliation in Bradford (PA) before moving their player development contract to Olean for three seasons. Olean operated from 1939-62 and played at Bradner Stadium which was built in 1926. It's still in use today as host to a summer collegiate league team and local high school football.

<u>Managers:</u> Paul Owens (1956-1957), Benny Zientara (1958).

Team Notes: (1956) Player-manager Owens led the league in hitting (.368) ... it was the 32-year-old's first season in the Phillies organization. (1957), another batting title (.407). He later became the legendary "Pope", the architect of the 1980 World Champion Phillies.

Paul Owens – Courtesy of Phillies

Tifton Phillies – Class D – 1956 - Tifton, GA

The second iteration of the Georgia-Florida League (GFL - 1946-1958) saw three different Phillies affiliations from 1956 to 1958. The Phillies signed a one-year player development contract with Tifton which had joined the league in 1949 as an independent club named the Blue Sox. They played their games at Eve Park.

Managers: Wes Griffin, Eddie Miller.

Tampa Tarpons – Class D – 1957-1960 -Tampa, FL

The Tampa Smokers professional baseball club was founded in 1919 as a charter member of the newly formed Florida State League (FSL) and lasted thru 1954. The Tarpons franchise was born in 1955 to replace the Smokers and began play in a brand-new venue, Al Lopez Field. They played as an independent team till 1957 when the Phillies became their first affiliated sponsor. The Fightins' franchise alignment stayed till the end of the 1960 season.

Managers: Charlie Gassaway (1957-59), Moose Johnson (1960)

Team Notes: (1957) Defeated the Palatka Red Legs in the Championship Series following an 84-54 regular season record. (1959) Also finished in first place (78-55) but lost in the Championship Series to the St. Petersburg Saints.

Johnson City Phillies-Class D-1957-1960-Johnson City, TN

Professional baseball in Johnson City dates back to 1910 as a member of the Appalachian League but the first affiliation was in 1939 with the St Louis Cardinals. In 1956 the Appalachian League went on a one-year hiatus but when the 1957 season opened the Phillies entered into an affiliation agreement. They played as the Phillies thru the 1960 season. They played at Keystone Park Field (built 1908) which is still in use today as TVA Credit Union Park. The Cardinals returned in 1974 and remain in a player development partnership.

Managers: Ben Taylor (1957), Eddie Lyons (1958-59), Benjamin Tompkins (1960).

Brunswick Phillies-Class D-1957-1958-Brunswick, GA

The Georgia-Florida League Phillies began in 1957 in Moultrie but moved to Brunswick, GA on June 1st. The Phillies played in Brunswick thru the 1958 season when the league folded. They played at Edo Miller Park which remains in use today by local school teams.

Managers: Benny Zientara (1957), Carl Howerton (1958).

Elmira Pioneers-Class D-1959-1961-Elmira, NY

The Elmira Pioneers pro franchise dates back to 1885. The Phillies played there three years as members of the New York-Penn League. They played at Dunn Field which was built in 1939 and remains in use today by a summer collegiate team. The franchise moved to Lowell, MA in 1995 (Lowell Spinners).

Managers: Andy Seminick (1959), Jack Phillips (1960), Moose Johnson (1961)

Team Notes: (1960) 18-year-old Dick Allen began his pro career as a shortstop and hit .281 in 320 AB's with 8 home runs and 42 RBI. Went on to what I consider a Hall of Fame 15-year, big-league career with the Phillies, Cardinals, Dodgers, White Sox, and Athletics. 19-year-old 1B Hank Allen, Dick's brother, also made his pro debut and hit .261 in 456 AB's. Went on to play in seven big-league seasons with the Senators, Brewers, and White Sox and then a long career as a scout.

Dothan Phillies -Class D-1961-1962-Dothan, AL

Dothan had minor league teams in the Alabama-Florida League or versions thereof beginning in 1936. The league existed for 24 years and Dothan was represented with a franchise for all but one of its seasons. The Phillies were in Dothan for two seasons before both the franchise and the league came to an end after the 1962 season. They played at Wiregrass Memorial Stadium which remains in use today as a municipal softball field.

Managers: Bob Wellman (1961), Moose Johnson (1962)

Team Notes: (1961) 18-year-old SS Mike Marshall made his pro debut by hitting 264 in 522 AB's with 7 home runs and 51 RBI. He would switch to pitching in 1965 which led to a 14-year, big-league career that included winning a Cy Young Award with the 1974 LA Dodgers.

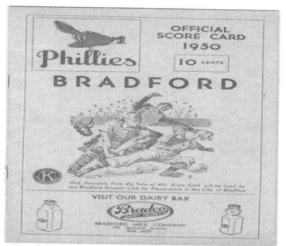

Bradford, PA, Blue Wings scorecard: Bob Warrington

Green Bay, WI, Joannes Stadium: Charles O'Reilly

337

Johnson City, TV, Keystone Park Field: Charles O'Reilly

Mattoon, IL, Phillies, Dallas Green's pro debut: Phillies

Olean, NY, Bradner Stadium: Charles O'Reilly

Appleton, WI, Goodland Field: Charles O'Reilly

339

Carbondale, PA, Russell Park: Kevin Colgan

Elmira, NY, Dunn Field: Charles O'Reilly

Phun and Games

Attending a minor league game is more than just baseball. There's a true emphasis on entertainment and fan interaction. At each of the Phillies minor league affiliates, the fan experience is highlighted and there's just as much action between innings as there is on the field during the game. There are mascots, on-field races, contests, and fan participation events ... all good fun that makes the experience all the more memorable. It's engaging and brings smiles to many faces ... it's all part of it!

Buster – Blue Claws Mascot – Michael Dill

Lakewood Eyeball" Race – Michael Dill

343

The Berm in Lakewood – Michael Dill

Funnel Cakes – Lakewood – Michael Dill

Phinley - Clearwater Threshers Mascot – Mark Wylie

Austin Listi & Bat Boy Dog at Threshers game – Mark Wylie

Uniform auction – Clearwater – Mark Wylie

Frenchy's Pavilion – Clearwater – Mark Wylie

Crazy Hot Dog Vendor – Reading – George Youngs Jr

Vegetable Race – Reading – Michael Dill

Photo by George Youngs Jr

Reading Mascots – George Youngs Jr

Ferris and FiFi – Iron Pigs Mascots – Cheryl Pursell

Lehigh Valley Between Innings Race – Cheryl Pursell

The Path Forward

In 1963 Minor League Baseball was re-structured into three basic classifications, AAA, AA and A levels of play. Adjustments were made over the years since. e.g. splitting the A level into the Advanced and Low A levels. The concept of short-season leagues was introduced in 1965 with rookie and international leagues also emerging and playing abbreviated game schedules.

In 2020 the structure was altered once again. Short-season leagues were disbanded as were Rookie levels of play with the exception of training complex based leagues. Limitations were placed on each organization to four full season teams only while the number of lower level camp based teams remained arbitrary. Limitations were also imposed on the maximum number of minor league players each organization can have rather than leaving that arbitrary.

The Phillies initial affiliates under the new structure remained the same however Clearwater and Lakewood switched levels within the A classification ... beginning in 2021 Lehigh Valley (AAA), Reading (AA), Jersey Shore (Advanced A) and Clearwater (Low A). The club will also field training complex based teams in both Clearwater and the Dominican.

More history to be written as minor league baseball returns to action adding to the already rich and lengthy tradition of player development and community relationships previously built. It's pro baseball at its core ... Happy Day, Happy Baseball !

About the Authors:

Dick Allen and Larry Shenk

Larry "The Baron" Shenk joined the Phillies organization in October 1963 as Director of public relations and was named Vice President,Public Relations, in 1981. After 44 years as the head of the PR Department, "The Baron" took on an advisory role in 2008 as Vice President, Alumni Relations and Team Historian. He officially retired following the 2015 baseball season. He's continued writing his "Phillies Insider" blog on phillies.com/alumni and has his own twitter @ShenkLarry. "The Phillies are my hobby. I don't play golf, can't swim, won't skydive or wrestle alligators."

Steve Potter

Steve Potter is the site owner and sole writer of the baseball blog Philliesbaseballfan.com also known as Phillies – A Fan's View on Facebook. He's a lifelong Phillies fan who retired from corporate life in 2015, moved to the Clearwater area from the Philly suburbs along with his wife Barb, and has been a daily fixture at Carpenter Complex since then … observing and writing about the Phillies. He's published nine books and initiated the Phillies Annual Minor League Digest in 2016. "Phillies Baseball is my passion … that's why every day is a Happy Day and Happy Baseball."

Editor:

Jim Peyton is the lead writer for Phuturephillies.com. Jim's site covers the Phillies' minor leagues each day, it is the foremost fan interactive site in that regard.

Photo Contributors

Mark Wylie – a Clearwater area resident who's been taking photos of the Phillies Minor League Players in action for multiple years.

Cheryl Pursell – Cheryl contributes her photos during the season to both the Lehigh Valley IronPigs and the Reading Fightins. You can follow her on Twitter at @CherylPursell

Michael Dill – the official team photographer for the Lakewood BlueClaws. His website for photography services is michaeldillphotography.com

George Youngs Jr – the official team photographer for the Reading Fightin Phils. He also has a Facebook page where he displays his photos entitled "Reading Fightin Phils Friends"

Danie Berlingis – a season ticket holder for the Threshers who contributes her photos to the cause.

Casey Burns – a Clearwater resident who uses his lunch breaks from work to take great photos of the Phillies Gulf Coast League action.

Joe Stinger – a Phillies fan

Barb Potter – a Phillies fan

Dave Schofield, now retired. Former team photographer for Lakewood BlueClaws and Trenton Thunder. Did photography for other minor league teams; Yankees, Red Sox, and Phillies on the major league level.

Miles Kennedy official photographer of the Philadelphia Phillies, a fixture in spring training and at Citizens Bank Park.

Charles O'Reilly, a Clearwater Threshers season ticket holder, who provided images from his incredible website, charliesballparks.com.

Ballparkreviews.com is another amazing website that contributed ballpark images.

Marc Viquez, a contributing writer/photographer on stadiumjourney.com.

Michael Rinehart whose passion for minor league baseball is documented on californialeaguehistory.com.

Made in the USA
Middletown, DE
01 March 2021

34636616R00197